DADDY, COME OUT AND PLAY!

Daddy, Come Out and Play!

Inspiration for Leading and Nurturing Your Family

Dr. D. Michael Stewart

Covenant Communications, Inc.

Published by Covenant Communications, Inc.
American Fork, Utah

Copyright © 1994 by D. Michael Stewart
All rights reserved

Printed in the United States of America
First Printing: October 1994

01 00 99 98 97 96 95 94   10 9 8 7 6 5 4 3 2 1
Library of Congress Cataloging-in-publication Data
Stewart, d. Michael, 1939-
Daddy, come out and play! : inspiration for leading and nuturing
your family / D. Michael Stewart
p. cm.
ISBN 1-55503-755-0 (pbk.) : $7.95
1. Fatherhood. 2. Fatherhood--Religious aspects--Christianity.
3. Parenting. I. Title.
HQ756.S819 1994
306.874'2--dc20

TABLE OF CONTENTS

Appreciation vii
The Parable of the Father ix
Preface xi
Introduction xiii
Chapter 1 The True Provider 1
Chapter 2 The Invisible Father...................................... 5
Chapter 3 Serving Your Child—Rare,
    Well Done, and Not So Hot 11
Chapter 4 Is This a Dream Daddy?
    Profile of a Successful Father 17
Chapter 5 From Faulty to Faultless Fathering............. 23
Chapter 6 Family Heirlooms....................................... 27
Chapter 7 Heir Conditioning...................................... 35
Chapter 8 Discipline, Example, and Rewards............. 43
Chapter 9 Does Dad Need a Time-out?
    Seeing Your Child on Five Dollars a Week 53
Chapter 10 Flexible Fathering and Children of Success 57
Chapter 11 Fathering from a Distance:
    Child Support Is More than a Monthly Check... 59
Chapter 12 Fathers of Divorce and Substitutes...................... 63
Chapter 13 Mrs. Dad... 67
Chapter 14 They'll Never Forget You:
    Hints of Endearment 71
Chapter 15 Daddy Dividends:
    Things I Was Near Enough to Hear 75
Chapter 16 Patience: The Fatherly Virtue 79
Chapter 17 Resolve to Come Out and Play................. 81
The Parable Retold.. 84
Notes 85
Suggested Reading 89

APPRECIATION

My circle of appreciation is wide. To Josephine Davis, Tina Braby, Terry Twitchell, Giles Florence, JoAnn Jolley, Christina Handy, Katie Graham, and Jeri Cartwright for insights, ideas, and preparation of this book.

To my bride, Betty Lou, for guiding me through the intersection of theory and practice and making it joyful to write a book for fathers, because she is so able as a mother.

To my children, the "significant seven," who make it easy to win the rewards of fathering and who continue to help me with my "homework."

Finally, to my father, who planted so well but died before the harvest. And to my friend, my mother, who preserved it standing alone.

The Parable of the Father

There is a tale, a parable of old men and young men who take turns tending a midnight fire that has burned as long as memory.

The fire protects the cave they call home and what they possess.
No one would dare let the fire go out.

The fire protects from the beast and the intruder.
The fire gives warmth and signals to other fire watchers that all is well at this fire.

Some leave the fire and go into the night.
Before they leave, they must place a log on the fire so that it continues to warm, protect, and signal that all is well.

No one would dare leave without feeding the fire.
No one would dare let the fire go out.

Preface

National statistics regarding child neglect and abuse, teenage pregnancy, and drug and alcohol dependency reveal a generation at risk and the tragic loss of human resources. To some it brings despair. Yet, despair is not a constructive response.

My reaction to the statistics is to ask if things are any worse today than in any previous generation. Is civilization sliding downward, or are we simply doing better reporting? Was the disillusionment of Henry David Thoreau, Socrates, or ancient Jeremiah well-founded? Did their generations outgrow their plight, or did the crisis deepen until mass revulsion brought reform or destruction? Will a better cycle return? New York City recently "solved" its social problems by hiring an additional 4,600 police officers. The U.S. annually spends $300 billion to deal with the consequences of such "solutions." There are better alternatives.

My concern is to focus on a lasting solution for our children—not to posture as a cynic or psychologist, but to act as an observer of both individual humans and communities which must pick up the pieces when families fall apart.

Many of my observations stem from my service as an elected official charged with delivering social and human services to hundreds of thousands of people and from my tenure as President of the National Association of Counties, where I observed enthusiastic national resolve yield feeble results in welding parents and children together. Insights gained from my discussions with hundreds of college youth as a history teacher and church and community youth leader spur me to speak up and out on the need for better fathering.

I have observed my own efforts as a father succeed and fail as my patience and attention have fluctuated. I could have used a good role model. My father died when I was just nine. I wish he had lived longer—at least to see me through my teen years. I needed him, even through my college years and into my early marriage and professional years! These pages are written to discover the model that I needed—that all children need. They are written for my nest of angels, my children, and for other nests.

Introduction

Several years ago, Bill Moyers produced a national news network program which focused on poverty and its relationship to teenage parenting. He concluded that a tragic, multi-generational cycle was becoming epidemic. In one interview, Moyers asked a jobless, listless young male how he felt about being responsible for the child he had just fathered and its mother. His response was poignant: "That was the best thing I ever accomplished—even though I don't know where they are." My heart cries for him. What can I do to lift him from his predicament, his low self-esteem, and his low aspiration? He symbolizes hundreds of thousands of youth who have become ciphers, zeros, rather than positive, contributing members of society.

Researchers and clinical psychologists have described the dysfunctional family as one that fails to meet the emotional needs of its members. They have concluded that 80% of all families have some dysfunction. This does not mean that the family is failing as a social institution—it simply means that the social illness that surrounds us is sapping its strength. Dysfunction leaches energy which could be retained to vanquish the monsters of modern living.

Youth and family dysfunction has been periodically attributed to social, moral, and technological changes. For example, in 1939 crime and delinquency were attributed to:

1. Lack of proper discipline in home and school.
2. Destructive toys and games.
3. Improper literature.
4. Movies, radio, and newspaper comic strips.

5. Alcohol.
6. Unsupervised groups, such as cellar clubs.
7. The automobile.
8. Improper home conditions.

However varied or periodic the causes of dysfunction, it is heartening to know that we can counter them with attentive parenting.

A child, when asked why a certain tree grew crooked, replied, "I suppose someone stepped on it when it was a little fellow." This book seeks a vision: that we can, as parents, and especially as fathers, straighten the crooked life which grows from social, moral, or technological evils, and above all from inadequate or unguided parenting. Robert Bly, in his stimulating book *Iron John: A Book About Men,* speaks of the stereotypical image of adult manhood adopted in popular culture, of how the image men are expected to live up to (or down to) is one we can no longer depend on. Bly states that "By the time a man is thirty-five he knows that the images of the right man, the tough man, the true man, which he received in high school do not work in life. Such a man is open to new visions of what a man is or could be."[1]

The luster and glow of good fathering can increase the human resource—a resource which must deal with challenge, change, and choice to survive. Transforming the father will transform the home, the nation, and the human race, whether in the inner city, suburbia, rural America, or across the world.

Good, effective fathering says to children that someone is looking after them. It says that someone wants to ensure that their fire remains burning, in their generation and in generations to come. So, here's to fathering in the pages within and the children without. Here's to making certain that the fire does not go out!

One
The True Provider

Six hours of spoken testimony, statistics, studies, and suggestions caused him to shift uneasily in his chair, yet he remained dead serious when he spoke. He was no showman. His gray hair and lined face testified to his age. Ernest Eberhardt had spent a lifetime counseling families, educators, and corporations. His words were profound:

> I am impressed with the information mustered by so many brilliant people addressing the deterioration of the American family. The conditions of child neglect, spouse abuse, vandalism, violence, and joblessness are clear. Some of you blame T.V., magazines, industry, etc. After forty years of studying, counseling, preparing, and observing successful families, I have concluded that nothing works as well as *having an effective father in the home.* Until we do something to prop up and prepare fathers for their role we shall never check the downward spiral of the family in America.[2]

The room was hushed. Dr. Eberhardt had dared say the difficult, the provocative, and the practical. The best minds in America had assembled together—a forum of state and local government leaders and private providers of human services. People left, pondering his words.

Fathers are as diverse in their parenting skills as in their surnames. Some fathers know how to parent, others wish they did, and still others could care less, rejecting accountability to and for their children. Diogenes, the ancient Greek, addressed this indifference when he said, "Strike the father whenever the child swears." He hoped to stimulate parental attention and change.

Often fathers, myself included, do damage in their anxiety to help a son or daughter. They become critics rather than counselors. As Joubert said, "Children have more need of models than critics."[3] It is to models of effective fathering and even failed fathering that we must turn in order to learn. It is time, as the ancient biblical prophet Malachi exhorted, to "turn the heart of the fathers to the children, and the heart of the children to their fathers" to stop the earth from being smitten with a curse.[4] Part of the curse of poor parenting today is streets and entire cities where lawlessness, violence, and bloodshed abound. The role of parents is to civilize and ensure that family members do not make war on each other and the community. Parents must prevent children from declining into savagery.

It can be argued that the world's problems, and specifically youth and home problems, do not stem solely from poverty or economic recession. Many who suffer such hardship still enjoy positive family relationships. Certainly, poverty can negatively impact a family; however, most people transcend these conditions when their mental, emotional, and spiritual needs are met. Columnist William Raspberry calls attention to Chester Finn's biting observation that most of the awful things that happen to those who constitute America's underclass are less the result of inadequate government intervention than of their own disastrous behavior, suggesting that no government policy or program will do much good unless they change their behavior.[5]

The skills of coping and adjusting to meet life's challenges are most effectively learned at home from parents or other strong role models. "An ounce of mother is worth a pound of priest," says the Spanish proverb. It can likewise be said that a pound of effective fathering is worth a carload of cops!

Dysfunction can surface at any stage in life, becoming an emotional and mental Achilles heel or Siegfried's shoulder. Such vulnerability can expose the whole person or even entire families to lasting emotional damage. Tragically, the unremedied vulnerabilities of one generation often become the next generation's birthright. For instance, a young man with emotional wounds inflicted by his parents recently committed a courthouse slaying in Salt Lake City. The young man's nephew watched the carnage from a distance, mesmerized, himself about to become the third generation of emotional illness in the family.

The optimistic view of social development suggests that it is the obligation of the next generation to stand on the shoulders of the current generation and do better. Willard F. Rockwell, chairman of Rockwell International, said:

> I have always heard that if the son isn't abler than the father there's something wrong with either the son or the father. I have worked like blazes all my life to prove there's nothing wrong with my old man.[6]

Whether it is a death row inmate or Willard Rockwell, the disparity in what results from strong and weak fathering models is becoming increasingly apparent.

Good fathering is never completed. When Wall Street financier Bernard Baruch made his first million dollars, he ran to tell his father. His father was not impressed. Bernard blurted out, "But Dad, I am not even thirty and I have already made my first million—and you are not happy!" His father replied, "No, my son. I am not impressed. What I want to know is, how will you spend the money you have earned?"[7] The father continued to teach his adult son lessons on values and philanthropy which he retained throughout his life and which guided his significant philanthropic inclination.

It is never too late to teach. It is never too late to become a model for a youth. There is wisdom in Mormon leader David O. McKay's words: "No success can compensate for failure in the home."

Becoming a father is not difficult, but *being* a father can be. Being a father requires commitment and initiative. Fatherhood is not a matter of qualification—it is a matter of desire, of caring enough to be a true provider. A true provider is much more than the source of a paycheck. He is an adviser, cheerleader, listener, teacher, and best friend. A true provider finds himself empowered, feeling peace and self-worth supplant guilt and self-doubt. He becomes more a model than a critic to his children. He completes his "homework" and makes the grade to nurture an effective, functioning family.

An effective father seeks for, cares about, and promotes the well-being and happiness of his child. But how does one learn how to become an effective father? Today's society requires specialized or professional training for most occupations. In fact, professionalization has become one of the defining characteristics of our time. Unfortunately, though, fathers have not had the benefit of such training. Evelyn Mills Duval makes the point in her book, *Marriage and Family Living,* that "Parents represent the last stand of the amateur. Every trade and profession has developed standards, has required study and practice and licensing before releasing the student into his work. Only one profession remains untutored and untrained—the bearing and rearing of our children." [8]

While professional training for fathers may be elusive, there are lessons to be drawn from the trials and errors of past fathers. Let us look at them.

Two
The Invisible Father

I have a wish for dads everywhere. It is for each of them to resist being an Invisible Father. A father who is committed to being visible adds dimensions of self-confidence, wholeness, and focus to his child's life.

The Invisible Father takes different forms. The first is Frank the Bank, the father who merely supplies his children with material assistance: food, clothing, shelter, education, and an allowance. Though present and paying, he is not emotionally involved or actively guiding his child. Ashley Montague describes him:

> Today, while the titular head of the family may still be the father, everyone knows that he is little more than the chairman, at most, the entertainment committee.[9]

Considering how difficult meeting the basic needs of a family is, just being Frank the Bank is no small task. Appreciation for a father's temporal contribution should be expressed. Frank the Bank's invisibility is sometimes accentuated because many mothers purchase the food and clothing, and hence are perceived as the providers of temporal necessities.

My seven-year-old, Emily, once asked me what I do with the money I make and if I was ever going to give the family anything other than allowances. I was startled, and immediately began a public relations campaign in my own behalf. I explained how badly the family needs me and how essential my paycheck is to what goes on in our family. It succeeded. Now Emily and her sisters ask more readily for financial assistance!

Divorce or separation can create a second form of the Invisible Father. Such a father, because he is often physically as well as emotionally distanced from his children, can become little more than an off-site Frank the Bank. Too often, both he and the on-site Frank the Bank leave the discipline, training, and caring needs of the family to the children's mother. She likely resents carrying the load and the lack of commitment to support her. Unfortunately, wives and mothers in this situation are deprived of knowing the difference a visible, active, emotionally involved father can make.

The third form of the Invisible Father is one who, through divorce, desertion, or indifference takes no active role in ensuring his child's welfare. He has emotionally, spiritually, and materially abandoned his children. He follows the path of the majority of males in the animal kingdom. One might say he has dropped a rung on the evolutionary ladder! He also doesn't know what he's missing.

In 1991, while we were involved in helping the Russian government make the transition to democracy, my wife and I visited some Russian schools. We asked a half-dozen youths who had been exchange students in New England what they enjoyed best and least about America and what some major differences were. Beyond their love for chewing gum and soft drinks was a response that startled me. "In America," they said, "we seldom saw our American fathers. They were all absorbed in their work and business. While in Russia, we see our fathers, we converse a lot and do a lot with them."

Children everywhere want a visible father. They notice the strength, presence, and support of a father, but may not readily vocalize it—at least not as well as the school child who wrote an essay on the Quakers, saying, "Quakers are very meek, quaint people who never fight or answer back. My father is a Quaker, but my mother is not." Children and youth need and want visible fathers. We know better than ever that a strong, loving father is indispensable to a child's harmonious psychological development.

Why should you be a visible, active father? If you are a father who vacillates between being a proactive force for good in your child's life and retreating to inactivity and invisibility, consider the following:

1. Seventy percent of the boys in long-term correctional facilities grew up without a father, according to David Blankenhorn, President of the American Institute of Values.
2. Scholars have concluded that the father's presence or absence, not race or income, most influences whether an urban at-risk child falls victim to poverty and dysfunction. My experience as an elected official and director of welfare and family services confirms this conclusion. I have seen thousands of families slip into or rise above poverty, all depending on whether the father commits himself to his family's well-being.
3. Children who benefit from strong, loving relationships with their fathers are more likely to enjoy healthy, fulfilling relationships with their spouses.
4. The instance of child abuse and neglect increases when biological fathers are removed from the home.
5. Nobody teaches a boy to be a father except his dad. It is an imitated skill. Too often, we give more attention to driver training than parental training.
6. A mother can teach a child kindness and cleanliness, but only a man can teach manhood. Fathers are necessary to raising children: they tickle, roughhouse, and encourage risk-taking when mothers emphasize being careful. At the playground, mothers caution, "Be careful as you climb," while fathers holler, "Go

all the way to the top!" Fathers push children to their limits. A child needs the balance that both mother and father bring.
7. Children who lack a visible relationship with their father often, like salmon, spend a good portion of their lives trying to find their origins.

I believe fathers can do things for children that others would not dare to. I asked a talented national consultant in land use planning what he liked about his dad, who was his business partner. He responded:

> I love his talent, his example, his providing for me and my sisters, his invitation to join him in the business. But the thing that stands out is the day when I lost a water rocket on the roof of an apartment complex near our home. I asked the bigger boys to climb up and get it. They were scared. I asked a big scrappy Vietnam vet to do it, but even he was afraid of heights. I even offered them a little money. Still no takers. I finally went home and told my dad. He came, climbed up the fire escape ladder, and, clinging to the sides of the building, retrieved the rocket as everyone looked on. He came down to a roar of approval from my friends. I then concluded that a dad can do things that no one else can do.[10]

Why else should a father be visible for his children? Why else be a better dad? Let me list a few reasons.

- Your child is the most valuable gift you will ever receive, even though he or she will grow up and eventually go his or her own way. Your child is a treasure that will be continually replenishing itself over the years.
- Your involvement will build your child's self-esteem and increase her or his potential for personal success.
- A healthy father-child relationship will impart joy from association and pride in continuity from one generation to the next. Neighbors may not hear what

a father says to his child, but it will most certainly be heard by generations to come.
- In the twilight of your life, feelings of companionship and inner peace will come from work well done—work that only you could do for your own children.
- Your loving example will help your child relate better with his or her spouse and children, thus perpetuating and replenishing the treasure.

How does one become a visible father when apparently so many fathers fail to do so, claiming to be at a disadvantage because they themselves lacked strong father models as children? The reason both you and I can do it is simple: Desire combined with strong resolve makes all things possible. You need only to want to be a good father and begin with a vision of what you want in your relationship with your child. Time is on your side. Fathering skills are learned by example or from models. Seek out and practice the habits of good father models. You will learn their skills. In nearly every human endeavor, a conscious and deliberate effort sustained over a period of time (21 days) will form a new habit.

Personal experience has taught me the value of developing positive fathering habits. Several years ago, my son was relating an exciting thing that had occurred during his day. I noticed that he looked only at his mother while talking and not at me. I interrupted and sharply said, "Why don't you look at me too when you talk?" He hesitated and answered, "Dad, perhaps if you were kinder I would look at you, but I don't like to see you when you're not kind." I was stunned. He was right. I, like many, am still working to improve my fathering skills. I want to be more visible in my son's eyes as well as in his life.

It is important that dads nurture strong, loving relationships with their children. We must change the social perception that a good father is an exception. In 1991, the *Chicago Sun Times* reported that eighty percent of fathers want to be more involved in the lives of their children. This response contrasted sharply with results from earlier polls, which showed money and the esteem of peers to be fathers' highest priorities. More often than not, fathers want to take an active, visible role in their children's rearing and learn better fathering skills. Being a good father is not a matter of talent, but of effort. The only prerequisites are desire and commitment.

My daughter recently told me the tragic story of a young acquaintance of hers. His father had formed a new family some years after divorcing his mother. The young man was a handsome, clean, robust, and athletic twenty-one-year-old, yet my daughter recalled how she had seen him ask his mother with tear-filled eyes and a voice choked with emotion, "Mom, oh Mom, why doesn't Dad pay any attention to me?" A few weeks later, while skiing, an avalanche swept him to his death.

I have often thought of this young man's heart-wrenching cry for his father. I wonder if his father knows how his son yearned to associate with him, how he longed for even the least bit of gentle counsel and approval from him. That father may never realize what both he and his son missed. Fathers everywhere must hear their sons' and daughters' cries for a visible, active father. They must assume a central role in their children's lives for the benefit of themselves, their children, and the generations to come.

Three
Serving Your Child—Rare, Well Done, and Not So Hot

The father-child relationship has been the subject of the world's best literature. It took center stage when the biblical prophet Abraham laid his son Isaac at the sacrificial altar, struggling to show his son the importance of obeying a higher law. We've read of Jacob's wrenching loss of his son Joseph, whose industry and integrity eventually preserved his father's household from starvation. Lesser-known men have also served as springboards for their children's success. Lyman Beecher insisted that his daughter read Sir Walter Scott. She did, and it set her mind ablaze. In time, Harriet Beecher Stowe wrote *Uncle Tom's Cabin,* the novel that foreshadowed the death knell of slavery in the United States. And the father's role as protector and provider has never been more poignantly defined than by the image of Joseph leading his donkey down a dusty Judean road, searching for shelter and food for Mary, who would that night bear the Christ child. Fathers past and present identify with the uncertainty Joseph must have felt in those anxious hours.

Ironically, fathers can strive to do all in their power to provide safety and certainty for their children and still fail to meet their most simple but deepest needs. Even the Presidents of the United States struggle to meet their children's needs.

President Calvin Coolidge's son suffered an injury from a fall on the White House tennis court. Dying from blood poisoning, the boy cried, "Daddy, do something for me! You are the President of the United States!" "Oh Daddy, do something for me!" is a cry echoed by children everywhere.

A zealous father urging a child to action sometimes oversteers his child. A father's firm but gentle guidance might have helped young Winston Churchill to follow a smoother course in his early years. Writing to his son Winston, Lord Randolph Churchill said:

> Never have I received a good report of you from your teachers. Always behind, never applying. You will be a failure in life just as they report to me. [11]

Young Winston's later career as the prime minister who led Britain through World War II disproved his father's skepticism. Had Lord Randolph Churchill spent more time with his son, he might have noted his son's leadership traits. In spite of his estrangement from his father, Winston was successful. Would that all young men could turn out so!

Children need more praise and less criticism. Adele Peck, who worked as a counselor for thirty years in the U.S. penal system, noted that rarely had a chronic offender, whether male or female, received any kind words or encouragement while growing up. Seldom praised for positive behavior, they simply turned to behavior which brought them attention, regardless of the negative consequences.

Adele Peck looked deep inside these unpraised and unappreciated youths and found moments of success in their past that she could applaud. She used these moments of hope to build the youths' self-esteem and persuade them that they could move on in a more positive, constructive direction.

Successful fathering is not always easy. Love and commitment are easier to give when they are reciprocated. Reciprocation on the part of the child will hopefully occur as a parent persists with different approaches and as the child matures. Even after a child leaves home, their father's love and attention will continue to positively influence his or her life. Samuel Johnson, the renowned British lexicographer who assembled the English dictionary, wrote of his father's sickbed request to have Samuel take his place hawking magazines and books. Although he knew his father was ill and although he loved his father, Samuel nevertheless let pride and embarrassment dissuade him from fulfilling his father's wish. Years later, out of respect for his father and remorse for disappointing him, Samuel took his umbrella and returned to the scene to holler, "Books for sale, books for sale!" to startled passers-by. This softened the remorse he felt for letting his father down.

I, too, had an experience similar to Johnson's. One summer night, while sleeping in our backyard, my brother and I succumbed to youthful curiosity and spied on our unsuspecting sister. My brother was in the tree and I was on the ground. In our distraction, we failed to notice our father standing a short distance away. He called to me. I was quick to defend my brother, saying he was in the tree peeking into a robin's nest counting the eggs. Father listened, his eyes searching deeply into mine. He was silent. I knew that he knew I was lying. I was left to struggle with the searing guilt of lying to my father. I never mustered the courage to confess the lie and to seek his pardon, and he died within a year. Getting down from that high tree was much easier than letting my father down. I wished for some kind of pardon. Yes, sometimes fathers and sons let each other down.

Fathers are often the people to whom we owe the most, but they rarely remind us of our debts. They send no bills and rarely ask for reimbursement. Edgar Guest once described such a father:

> I knew he was as fine a dad as any boy ever had—kind, cheerful, humorous, hard-working and patient, severe at times over my indifferent efforts and boyish carelessness, but severe always with a kindly purpose and very proud of his

children whenever they did anything that seemed worthy. What I didn't know until too late was the depth of his wisdom and the magnitude of his sacrifice. [12]

These are the words of comfort and commendation that fathers hope to deserve from their children. An occasional word or letter of gratitude from a child goes far. The pressure of a difficult day, a faltering business, or an automobile that won't start make harmonious family living and fathering difficult. In a sometimes hectic and confusing world, young men and women can find a wealth of resources, insight, and experience in conversation with their fathers.

Friendship based on accountability and genuine interest strengthens the lines of communication between fathers and children. Rather than telling our older children to talk to us, my wife and I leave the bedroom door open as an invitation to the children to stop in. Their spirit is relaxed and open when they drop on our bed to recount the day's events.

I imagine that Saul enjoyed an open, trusting relationship with his father, Kish, who sent Saul to search for a lost donkey. After searching for the donkey unsuccessfully for a prolonged period, Saul's thoughts turned to his father and the anxiety he imagined his absence must be causing him. Saul told his servant, "Come, let us return lest my father begin to worry more about me than he does for the donkey." Such sensitivity about parental concern caused a writer in Saul's day to describe Saul as "a choice young man, and a goodly: and there was not among the children of Israel a godlier person than he: from his shoulders and upward he was higher than any of the people."[13] The state of our society would certainly improve if more youth followed Saul's example.

Almost invariably, fathers conclude after some reflection that parenting is more difficult than they had imagined. Such was the opinion of my 89-year-old mother-in-law who, when commenting on a troubled teenager in the family, observed, "Growing up is as hard as growing old." Her reflection offers much-needed reassurance that others understand the struggles of parenting.

Author Willie Morris writes of the rewards that flow from the parent-child relationship:

> I have a memory of going with a comrade now living in New England to a nursing home in his native South to bring back his aged father to live with his family. The pristine joy in the old man's face when the son came into his room to take him home, and their affectionate embrace, were to me an imperishable affirmation.[14]

Our struggles as fathers dim when compared with the promise of experiencing such an "imperishable affirmation" with our children. This strong emotional tie between a father and child, says clinical psychologist Dr. Terry Lee Burnham, "keeps kids out of trouble."[15]

Four
Is This a Dream Daddy?
Profile of a Successful Father

Once, while watching the *Nutcracker* ballet, my six-year-old daughter turned to me and said, "Is this a dream, Daddy?" I pondered the potential double meaning in her question: was it "a dream, Daddy," or "a dream daddy"? I reflected on how I would like to be a good model, a *dream daddy*, to see and be most everything my children need. Being a dream daddy requires attention and energy. Someone observed that "raising children is a complicated undertaking, like trying to understand the Trinity—Father, Son, and Wholly Confused." But, rather than be wholly confused, take heart. We can all acquire certain habits and practices of successful parenting that have been universally proven. What are they?

First, successful parents *strengthen their relationships through family activities.* Parents who commit to spend at least a minimum amount of time with their children on a regular, scheduled basis are more likely to succeed. The average parent spends less than ten minutes a day talking with each child. Time together on a regular basis allows for communication that builds strong relationships.

Setting aside time to read to a child, to go to a park, to plan a special dinner or day will help build a communicative rather than combative relationship.

Second, successful parents *establish rules and expectations* with input from the children. A child raised without rules and with little supervision is a candidate for juvenile delinquency. Parents do best when they are friendly but firm.

Third, successful parents *build self-esteem in their children.* Self-esteem can be developed within any child. Growing up is hard. At some point, every child suffers rejection or harsh treatment from peers. Labeling and name-calling lowers self-esteem and makes withstanding peer pressure difficult. To help ease growing pains, involve your children in noncompetitive activities, such as "nerd" football, checkers, or rug weaving. These allow children the opportunity to gain a better feeling about themselves.

Fourth, successful parents *help the family set achievable goals.* Working toward family goals helps family members learn to make correct decisions and helps them focus on their hopes and dreams. Children who have goals are less likely to get involved in negative or self-destructive activities.

Children and adults deserve the right to fail at some of their goals. Facing the reality of unmet goals can further our children's maturity if we help our children acknowledge that failure is a stepping-stone to success.

Fifth, successful families *have a strong set of values or a high degree of religious orientation.* These values help individuals reach beyond themselves and the immediate and present into the lives of others. They encourage a whole view of life—one centered on love for family and service to the community. An ethic of service teaches children an awareness of concerns outside their own. It fosters empathy and spurs the resolve to improve the human condition.

Sixth, successful families *speak warm praise and encouraging words.* Such words are:

"I really enjoy being with you."
"I enjoy your smile."
"Good for you, you know how to do it right!"
"Sensational!"

"I like that!"

"There you go—that's it!"

"Keep it up and you'll be a champion!"

Seventh, successful families *perform family "tune-ups."* Strong families counsel together, assess their situation periodically, and ask: "How are we doing?" Strong families seek genuine improvement, taking the attitude that the family, marriage, or child is worth something and things need to be tuned up to get better MPG—better *marriage, parents,* and children *growth.* In matters where little agreement is reached or things are at an impasse, the family might need to involve a mediator, religious leader, relative, or competent counselor. In informal family councils, the parties just *listen* to each other without attempting to explain their behavior. Such sessions often bring to light troublesome issues which were formerly unuttered and unresolved.

To make tune-ups work, families must try to see things from the speaker's perspective. To do this, everyone must listen without anticipating a reply and stay in the speaker's head. Listeners should describe what the speaker has expressed without passing judgment, helping reassure the speaker that they have paid attention. The speaker can then leave the discussion feeling he or she has been heard, allowing for a complete tune-up session or "home repair."

My children caught my attention in a tune-up session in which each of them expressed their feelings toward me. What proved most difficult for me wasn't hearing the lament in their voices, but rather trying to paraphrase back to them what they felt and expressed. For example, I would paraphrase their feelings, saying, "You feel irritated when I honk the horn in the driveway while waiting for everyone to come so we can leave," and they would answer, "Yes, I feel honking the horn demeans me and I wish you would be patient and not do it!" I'd continue, "You think I'm okay until I do that?" To my relief, they would answer, "Yes."

You can schedule tune-ups regularly or as needed. To ensure

sufficient interest, a nonjudgmental, nonpunitive atmosphere should prevail. Tune-up sessions clarify situations that parents can understand and remedy. In tune-up sessions, children might reveal the following issues:

- Their parents spend too little time with them either socially or in doing homework.
- They resent their parents arguing in their presence.
- Their parents give them too little to do. Wise parents learn that they must provide outlets for their children. Animals provide wonderful outlets for children, teaching them caring, affection, and responsibility.

I have noted that an attitude of respect, not control, flows from successful tune-up sessions.

The issues of respect and control bring us to an examination of two types of strong, influential fathers: the authori*tative* father and the authori*tarian* father. Successful fathers are authoritative. They proceed with confidence, involving family members in setting standards of behavior and discipline. Authoritative fathers win respect through fairness and do not want their children to perceive them as omnipotent and omniscient. Rather, they hope to be careful listeners who judge and act with fairness. An authoritative father respects his children's right to make mistakes. He simply strives to be loving as well as firm.

The authoritative father assumes that his role is one of trust in the gentle exercise of parental prerogatives. He seeks to persuade and reason with his children without raising his voice even when his patience is long exhausted. He has learned, as someone once wrote, that nothing is so powerful as real gentleness, and nothing is so gentle as genuine power. Authoritative fathers act with the following set of credos in mind:

1. I respect my children.
2. I value my children's opinions.
3. I shall involve my children in setting the rules for our home.
4. I have confidence in my children. I shall trust them completely to comply with family guidelines.
5. I make mistakes, and therefore must allow my children to also. I will protect them from big mistakes and pitfalls as well as I can, but will also allow them to face the consequences of poor decisions.

These credos contrast starkly with the attitude of an authoritarian father, who prefers the iron-hand approach to child rearing. His approach seems easiest while children are small but wears thin by the time they reach their teens. An authoritarian father believes it is "his home" instead of "our home." He insists, "This is the way it is here, since I'm your dad," instead of saying, "Responsible fathers care and feel this way." He demands that his children never fail and feels they should have little say in matters. In a nutshell, the authoritarian father creates a non-participative family. He stifles his children's initiative and contributions, and thus lowers their sense of self-worth.

Authoritarian fathers eventually fail or fade away, frustrated and forlorn like an authoritarian, feeble third-world government. It is no wonder that corporations which practice authoritarian management see profits, sales, and morale flag until they eventually fail. A participative, authoritative style of leadership at home, as well as in government and in the business world, far surpasses the faithless, unimaginative authoritarian style.

Becoming a successful father need not be an elusive dream. Every father committed to the well-being and happiness of his family has the potential to become a "dream daddy."

Five
From Faulty to Faultless Fathering

Ring Lardner wrote, "The family you come from isn't as important as the family you are going to have."[16] Fathers ought to be less concerned about where they came from and more concerned about how they themselves perform as parents. They should focus their energy on the things they can do something about. This same sentiment was expressed anciently when one well-born Roman chided a lesser-born Roman, saying, "My ancestry is aristocratic and goes back generations and is directly traceable to me." The lesser-born Roman hesitated and softly answered, "Yes, that may be true. Your nobility, however, ends with you—and mine begins with me!"

A history of great fathering can begin with you. You can become a *founding* father rather than a floundering father. A founding father gives his family a legacy of nurturing and love. He extends strong emotional support to his sons and daughters as they face their future. He resolves to help them find joy in the journey of life.

Threats to the basic family structure that have arisen in recent history underscore the importance of being a founding father. The relationships of fathers and sons in our current industrial- and service-oriented society differ vastly from those which existed in the agrarian society of years past, one in which families worked and conversed side by side. Exchanging that way of life for a higher standard of living and an automated, dust-free environment has led to the weakening of interfamily and intrafamily communication. When Eli Whitney began to manufacture gun barrels in 1793, little did he realize that his concept of interchangeable parts, the assembly line, and the factory system would revolutionize the family as well as industrial production. The loss of informal conversation and personal interaction began to weaken the family fabric necessary to sustain a healthy industrial society.

The industrial revolution also weakened the classical tradition of passing down the crafts and skills of one generation to the next. Likewise, the Judeo-Christian precept of honoring one's father and mother fell victim to the sweeping societal changes ushered in with the shift to an industrial- and service-centered economy. People still worked hard, long days, but not with their families. Their children were not around them. Impersonal, monotonous, routine labor characterized the work site, which became bereft of conversation and familiarity with the dreams and aspirations of ancestors.

Accompanying the disassembling of the family has been the advent of labor-saving devices such as dishwashers, washers and dryers, television, and the automobile. These "advancements" endangered family-strengthening activities such as side-by-side work and conversation. Disconnection and dysfunction began to occur. Father and child became detached. Fathers, historically accessible role models for their children, became less visible in family life and thus began to hold less influence over the lives of their children.

To avoid becoming casualties of modernization, fathers must seek to turn around their relationships with their children. Some fathers are learning this the hard way, facing the distrust and disrespect that years of neglect have engendered in their children. Their children's words haunt them: "Dad, you say we are going to do that, but we never do!" Fathers must learn what every good scoutmaster knows: You never, never cancel a camping trip, come rain, snow, or work. Promises of time spent together raise your children's expectations. When you burst their bubble, when you disappoint them, you dampen their enthusiasm and risk impairing a trusted relationship. Fathers must schedule regular blocks of time dedicated to their sons and daughters. Fathers are finding that the glow of professional success pales in comparison to the joy that comes from healthy relationships with their sons and daughters.

Fathers who place their professions first often attempt to compensate by showering their children with material possessions. Such "gifts" require little effort and leave their recipients without that which they most want or need: their father! Children need their father's presence, not his presents! They need the praise, discipline, and guidance essential to their successful passage through life.

Fortunately, popular notions of what fathering is about are changing. Many fathers are assuming tasks at home in the kitchen and the nursery. Their children are supplanting their professions as their first priority. These days, fathers can be seen jogging and running while pushing strollers, some shortening their stride so another child can keep up.

Several years ago, my sensitivity was enhanced when my wife urged me to rearrange the children's bedrooms. My nine-year-old son's desk was surprisingly heavy. I inspected the drawers, which were filled with everything imaginable. From my perspective, the items in the drawers had little worth. My first impulse was to sort, select, and dispose. All of a sudden I was struck by a searing feeling. What right did I have to determine what was of value to a nine-year-old? My guilt came first as a father, and then as a constitutional historian who was about to violate the rights of privacy and private property.

That experience, coupled with another some years later, reinforced my growing sensitivity. I offered to pay my son for helping me with some Saturday work. We worked side by side during the day and talked casually. When we were finished, I went to pay him. He declined to take the money, saying, "No thank you, Father, it was fun just to be with you." I insisted. He responded, "Let's do it this way. You can pay me when I work alone, but when we work together it's for free!" I resolved that day to become more like my son: willing, caring, friendly. His attitude fanned my desire to be a better father.

Six

Family Heirlooms

Concern about effective parenting is not new to mankind. Socrates scolded the Athenians for not taking more pride in the directing of children in his day:

> What mean ye fellow Athenians that ye turn every stone to scrape wealth together and take so little care of your children to whom one day ye must relinquish all?[17]

Socrates' contemporary, the Roman mother Cornelia, was visited by a fashionable lady who boasted of her own fine robes and jewels. "You must have jewels too?" the lady asked. "Show me your finest." Cornelia left the room and returned with two little sons. Holding each by the hand, she said, "These are my jewels."

We can draw several messages from Socrates and Cornelia. Applying their outlooks to our time, we might say that when each father shows as much concern about his children's welfare and development as he does about his hunting dog, BMW, or the snell darter and spotted owl, the next generation will thrive.

Like most fathers, I am concerned about how my children feel about me. I was once sobered by one of my teenage daughter's honest observations. Confiding to her mother, she said, "Mother, I don't want to marry anyone who is as strong-willed as Dad." Her comment prompted me to rethink how I interact with my children. It caused me to think about how I am conditioning the next generation.

As a father, I am literally conditioning, determining the thoughts and attitudes my daughter carries into the future. Our heirs are profoundly influenced by the effectiveness of our fathering skills. William Livingston Larned, author of *Father Forgets*, shares a moment that strengthened his resolve to improve himself as a father:

> Listen, son, I am saying this to you as you lie asleep, one little paw crumpled under your cheek and the blond curls stickily wet on your damp forehead. I have stolen into your room alone. Just a few moments ago, as I sat reading my paper in the library, a hot, stifling wave of remorse swept over me. I could not resist it. Guiltily I came to your bedside.
>
> These were the things I was thinking, son: I had been cross to you. I scolded you as you were dressing for school because you gave your face merely a dab with a towel. I took you to task for not cleaning your shoes. I called out angrily when I found you had thrown some of your things on the floor.
>
> At breakfast, I found fault too. You spilled things. You gulped down your food. You put your elbows on the table. You spread butter too thick on your bread. And as you started off to play and I made for my train, you turned and waved a little hand and called, "Goodbye, Papa!" and I frowned and said in reply, "Hold your shoulders back!"
>
> Then it began all over again in the late afternoon. As I came up the hill road, I spied you down on your knees, playing marbles. There were holes in your stockings. I humiliated you before your boy friends, by making you march on ahead of me, back to the house. Stockings were expensive—and if you had to buy them you would be more careful. Imagine that, son, from a father! It was such a stupid, silly logic.

Daddy, Come Out and Play!

But do you remember, later, when I was reading in the library, how you came in softly, timidly, with a sort of hurt, hunted look in your eyes? When I glanced up, over my paper, impatient at the interruption, you hesitated at the door. "What is it you want?" I snapped.

You said nothing, but you ran across, gathering all your childish courage, in one tempestuous plunge, and threw your arms around my neck, and kissed me, again and again, and your small arms tightened with an affection that God had set blooming in your heart and which even neglect could not wither. And then you were gone, pattering up the stairs.

Well, son, it was shortly afterwards that my paper slipped from my hands and a terrible, sickening fear came over me. Suddenly I saw myself as I really was, in all my horrid selfishness, and I felt sick at heart.

What had habit been doing to me? The habit of complaining, of finding fault, of reprimanding—all these were my rewards to you for being a boy. It was not that I did not love you; it was that I expected so terribly much of youth. I was measuring you by the yardstick of my own years.

And there is so much that is good, and fine, and true in your character. You did not deserve my treatment of you, son. The little heart of you was as big as the dawn itself, over wide hills. All this was shown by your spontaneous impulse to rush in and kiss me goodnight. Nothing else matters tonight, son. I have come to your bedside in the darkness, and I have knelt here, choking with emotion and so ashamed!

It is a feeble atonement. I know you would not understand these things if I told them to you during your waking hours. Yet I must say what I am saying. I must burn sacrificial fires, alone, here in your own bedroom, and make free confession.

And I have prayed God to strengthen me in my new resolve. Tomorrow I will be a real daddy! I will keep saying, as if it were a ritual: "He is nothing but a boy—a little boy!"

I am afraid I have visualized you as a man. Yet I see you

now, son, crumpled and weary in your cot, I see that you are still a baby. Yesterday you were in your mother's arms, your head on her shoulder. I have asked too much, too much!

Dear boy! Dear little son! A penitent kneels at your infant shrine, here in the moonlight. I kiss the little fingers, and the damp forehead, and the yellow curls, and, if it were not for waking you, I would snatch you up and crush you to my breast.

Tears came and heartache and remorse and, I think, greater, deeper love, when you ran through the library door and wanted to kiss me.[18]

Whether a library door or garage door, a three-year-old or seventeen-year-old, the message is the same: We owe our children the best of what we are.

The Power of a Worthy Example

Children are heirs in more than just a legal sense. They inherit from parents more than mere property. They inherit what Luther Burbank describes as "All [their] predecessors' stored environment." Genetically and environmentally, we reflect everything that has gone before. While some people pass along great treasures or a life's accumulations, all will, if they have children, pass along genetic and environmental conditioning. How can one ensure that the best of what we are is passed on?

First, *set a worthy example*. As noted above, in the nineteenth century, Joseph Joubert wrote that "Children have more need of models than critics." His insight preceded several generations of research supporting the notion that youth, before the age of twelve, rely almost entirely upon a role model for education. In addition, during their teenage years, children need and depend on a role model to mature to well-balanced adulthood. Young men especially need to be welcomed by older men into the real world. Robert Bly relates the experience of Detroit's Chief of Police, who says the young men he arrests not only don't have any responsible, older man in the house, but that they have never even met one! Bly quotes Michael Meade, who says that gangs are simply groups of young men with no older men around them. Gang members try desperately to learn courage, family loyalty, and discipline from each other. It works for a few, but not for most.

A short time ago, I repeatedly told my ten-year-old to clean her room. I chided her for "hanging her clothes up on the floor." She smiled, stalled, and eventually made a light assault on the mountain, but without scaling the summit! Finally, in desperation, I went in, stood at her side, and helped her. Since that moment, she has done clean-up respectably. She needed less command and more instruction!

In another setting, a young woman was asked whose preaching had brought her to God. "It wasn't anybody's preaching," she responded, "it was my parents' practicing." A child needs less correction and more role modeling. The wag Josh Billings put it another way: "To bring up a child in the ways he should go, travel that way yourself once in a while."[19]

Colonel Calvin Jackson, helicopter test pilot and former pilot to Presidents Eisenhower and Kennedy, found himself at a mental and spiritual ebb in his career. He reflected on his father's struggle with a crippling disease. In spite of his disease, Calvin Jackson's father continued on crutches and puss-filled feet to voluntarily fill out and deliver church reports on a regular basis. That memory of his father brought Calvin the same habit of perseverance to continue his own demanding career. Children need models, not critics.

Youth with professionally successful or prominent fathers may struggle with feelings of needing to follow in their fathers' footsteps. Austin O'Malley felt that the worst thing that could happen to an ordinary man was to have an extraordinary father. The journal of Henry Clay's son reveals, "How difficult it is for a young tree to grow in the shade of an aged oak." As difficult as having a worthy, famous father model may be for some, it is clearly superior to having no model at all.

A father can draw as much strength and character from a child's example as a child can from a father's. During the One Hundred Years' War, the Swedish King Adolphus poised his army to destroy the city of Rottenburg, Germany. About to sound the attack, he suddenly observed the figure of a young boy on the wall above him. It reminded him of his own son far away at home. His heart was softened and destruction was averted.

Several hundred years later, in 1964, the teenage daughter of a religious representative was confronted by an East German Communist border guard. He was perfunctory, officious, and devoid of warmth. He asked, in a severe voice, whether she was going to follow her father in his religion. She pondered and responded, "Yes, I see all around me the need to do so. Yes, more than ever before I am going to follow his religion."[20] And she has done so with zeal. Such examples fill the unwritten history of the human race.

A worthy example provides an anchor and direction for youth. Actor and director Kevin Costner describes his father in tender terms:

> My dad was a tremendous influence on me, and I still talk to him nearly every day. He's the kind of guy that if he borrowed somebody's lawnmower, when he gave it back the tank was full of gas and the lawnmower was clean. He never missed anything I was part of . . . I want to be like my dad.[21]

Lydia Sigourney adds that "Whatever you would have your children become, strive to exhibit it in your own lives and conversation."[22]

A father's influence lingers long after he leaves the scene. Speaking at his father's funeral, Steven Craig described being stranded on a cliff high over a valley where he had gone on a solo hike. His desperate cries awakened his father, who immediately went to help. But his father could not negotiate the precarious trail leading to where he was stranded. Steven's father finally called, "I cannot come to where you are, but I can tell you where to step."²³ After painfully anxious moments, the boy safely reached his father's side. A father's strong example can serve as a lifelong guide to safe, fruitful pathways.

Seven
Heir Conditioning

A wise individual once observed that "There are only two lasting bequests we can hope to give to our children. One of these is roots and the other is wings."[24] What are the principles which build a worthy male role model? What is the key to successful "heir conditioning"? How do we give our children both roots and wings?

The Miracle of Motivation

Dealing with youth and children, instilling in them desire and motivation to achieve, are major undertakings. Motivation often becomes a matter of inspiration and individual perseverance. The concept of personal achievement is sufficient to motivate most adults. However, darker enticements such as fear and greed are also major sources of motivation for many of us.

Adults are rewarded personally by living up to their ideals and goals and the satisfaction of achieving them.

Children are similarly motivated. They seek after money, material gain, and parent and peer approval. Feelings of accomplishment spur all children to success and self-esteem. Some parents wisely withhold material gifts in order to avoid spoiling the child, giving gifts with measured restraint to engender appreciation and gratitude.

The varieties of effective motivation are as varied as children themselves. Some children take a dare; some develop desires based on feelings of caring; others seek to achieve in order to compete with or in spite of others. In all instances, personal motivation is vital to healthy self-perception and self-approval. Observant parents will assess what motivates their children and provide that motivation to help them flourish.

Teaching children to care about something is at the heart of motivation. A child with something to care about, something to do, and something to look forward to will thrive, be happy, and stay out of trouble. Methodist Bishop Wright, of Coos Bay, Oregon, unwittingly stimulated his sons in a novel way. One day the family discussion turned to the assertion that man would soon fly and be able to transport himself as quickly as the birds. The bishop said that God did not intend man to fly, and that had he so intended, he would have provided wings for him. Be that as it may, shortly afterwards he was transferred to North Carolina, where his own sons, Wilbur and Orville Wright, proved their father wrong and realized their dream of flying the first airplane.

Bishop Wright's "It can't be done" attitude likely steeled Wilbur and Orville's resolve to fulfill their dream. Whatever the motivational approach—encouragement, example, incentives, a dare, or even caring, reasoning patience—a child can develop desire and motivation.

Overcoming the Fear of Failure

Fear of failure or loss can be a form of motivation. If fear inspires action, even remedial action, rather than self-doubt, it is a useful tool. Children can gain self-confidence if they learn that mistakes or temporary failures are steps to learning and maturity, not dead-ends. Children must be taught to see failure as a process of achievement rather than as a reason not to even try.

It is helpful for a son or daughter to hear that father or mother made mistakes along the way. A candid discussion of pitfalls is invaluable and relieves anxiety. It calms a child to know that occasional failure is acceptable. Knowing that I did not learn to hopscotch and skip as readily as other grade-schoolers reassures my son that he is still okay.

Knowing that my own father succeeded and yet still struggled gives me hope. Just as Babe Ruth struck out 1301 times to hit 706 home runs, and just as Thomas Edison languished through numerous failed experiments before inventing the electric light bulb, so too will your children succeed if they view their failures as steps in a larger process of achievement.

The Mellow Voice of Encouragement

Genuine encouragement can kindle desire in a child. Children should be able to seek and find safe harbor in their fathers' arms. Unfortunately, children occasionally find that the world is kinder to them than are their parents. Fathers must ensure that this does not happen. Henry Ward Beecher wrote, "Whatever the mother says to the cradle goes all the way down to the coffin."

A nineteenth-century religious leader, Joseph Smith, found a resource in a father who comforted him and encouraged his purposes. Early in his life, Joseph had to undergo a gruesome operation to have an infected bone removed from his leg. Joseph, determined not to take whiskey as an anesthetic, requested only that his father hold him tightly in his arms.

Richard Rowley's son yearned to be a Boy Scout, an unlikely aspiration since the boy was a quadriplegic. Together, Richard and his son anguished over the camping and hiking requirements. Finally, Richard, with a stroke of inspiration, purchased a wheelbarrow, placed his son in it, gear and all, and pushed him along the trail wherever the troop went. His effort sustained the boy to his death nine years later. Richard Rowley's encouragement greatly enriched his son's short stay on earth.

"It's only a little farther," a father said to his son on a

Sunday afternoon walk. The child struggled on a little longer. The child asked his father how far a little farther was. "It is farther than you can see, but not as far as you can go," he answered. The soft encouragement on that afternoon blazed into the boy's memory and gave him courage as a man.

On another occasion, three musically talented sisters recalled with affection their father's attendance at scores of recitals. His hallmark was an approving, twinkling wink from the audience.

In small ways a word, a wink, a hand on the shoulder, or a hug sends the signal of encouragement, galvanizing a youth's confidence.

Tell Me I'm Important

Children long to know that their fathers consider them important. They need to be told they're somebody, not just anybody, to be called by name and told they're okay. Children showered with approval learn to live comfortably with themselves.

Much of a child's self-esteem is won in daily conversation. My seven-year-old ran into the kitchen from school and blurted out, "I'm the best reader in the second group—that makes me pretty good, Mom, doesn't it?!" Assurance after assurance and affirmation after affirmation form the long rope children pull themselves up with.

Fathers can reassure their children that they care by simply stating that they occasionally work late hours not just for professional advancement, but because they want to provide material necessities and make life pleasant for the family.

Dan Pursuit tells of the value of recognition and feeling important to a child:

> All children wear the sign: "I want to be important NOW!" Many of our juvenile delinquency problems arise because nobody reads the sign.[25]

Telling a child he or she is important and loved affirms their hope and desire to be loved and to love. Affirmations of love strengthen a child's self-worth and serve as the springboard to a successful, fulfilling future.

Words of Importance

A child gets the emotional "armor" from his parents to withstand kindergarten, says psychologist Victor Cline. Such armor is welded from right words and phrases spoken at the proper time. It is forged by refraining from speaking words that bruise self-confidence. Tether your tongue when the urge to criticize is tripping on your teeth. Strike the words "dumb" and "stupid" from your vocabulary and you will instantly boost your child's self-esteem and your self-control. Rather than saying, "Get it together," say, "Keep it together." The difference in meaning and perception is important. "Keep it together" communicates both your concern and your support.

The words a father uses when speaking to his child can be more relevant and important than those he or she hears from anyone else during the day. Significant research reveals that most children can weather the storm of peer pressure if they can fall back on a reassuring relationship with a parent, mentor, or teacher. Peer pressure, while a contributing factor in misbehavior, can be offset. You can address it by nurturing a positive parent-child relationship.

Ken Hubbard writes that a little kindness goes a long way, especially when it ought to stay at home. Praise and kindness at home work wonders in preparing a child to learn. You convey praise and kindness when:

- You praise a child for good work: for good schoolwork, for cleaning his or her room, or for progress in anything.
- You praise a child for effort spent, even though he or she may have fallen short of the goal or even failed.
- You praise a child in front of others, especially when he or she thinks you do not know they are present.
- You praise in original or different ways. Helpful

phrases might be, "The President of the United States is flying in to see your room because it is so clean," or "No Miss America ever had more grace under pressure than you had tonight," or "If Christopher Columbus were starting out for the New World, he'd choose you to be part of his crew!"
- You express your feelings with a handwritten note. Leave it in a lunchbox, on a pillow, or in any unexpected place.

Positive praise is like an emotional bank account. Psychologists tell us this account needs regular deposits of assurance to keep a healthy balance. When you criticize your child, you make a withdrawal from that account. A healthy child, like a healthy business, requires more deposits than withdrawals. A better balance means a thriving child.

Show Me I'm Important

"The best gift a father can give his child is his time," writes O. A. Bettista. Words of affection are important, but time spent together leaves tangible, vivid memories. "I know my mother loves me," said one teenager, "because she lets me lick the beaters when she bakes a cake." A father who plays catch, attends his son's game, or drives his daughter and her friends to a party is showing his love concretely. He conveys approval and invites conversation. It is in such moments that bonding and loyalty develop. George Herbert wrote well when he said, "One father is worth more than a hundred school masters."

Children need physical affection from their fathers. This fact is demonstrated in research conducted on the post-natal care of infants which showed that infants thrive and grow more vigorously when they are touched. Holding and hugging time, if it lasts for just a few seconds during your child's day, is akin to healing. Likewise, discipline is more effective for some children when a caring hand is placed on their shoulder, reassuring them that they are still loved.

Finally, let a child perform for you. Let them practice a talk, a school report, or a musical instrument in front of you. Three things result when you give this type of attention: the child learns a skill, increases his or her confidence, and learns that you care. By showing interest, not merely talking about it, you say to a child, "I'm your patron and your booster."

As a seven-year-old, my son helped carry the garbage cans to the street. Struggling with his can, he observed me carry a can in each hand. He exclaimed with obvious ambition, "Daddy, some day I will be a two-can man!" Upon occasion, I remember that my role is to encourage and show him he can be all he wants to become—even a two-can man.

Eight
Discipline, Example, and Rewards

Parenthood is not supposed to be a popularity contest. Children must be taught and corrected so they will learn the realities of life. It is far better for a loving father to discipline his child than to permit abusive, antisocial behavior to go unpunished, leaving it to be corrected by the community's criminal justice system.

Children want acceptance. Acceptance is particularly essential at the threshold of puberty, when children become unsure of themselves, self-critical, and are sabotaged by their own hormones. Every child is potentially at risk if not given strong, sensible direction. Children want to know what's right and will accept authority if it is clear and fair. With that in mind, a wise father will do the following:

- *He will discipline privately.* He will reduce the audience if a child or youth is in a rage or tantrum.
- *He will not be angry or volatile when he disciplines.* A wise father will wait until his anger subsides. President William H. Taft was in full emotional control when his son rebuked him in front of guests at the White House. "Bill, are you going to let that child talk to you like that?" said a friend. The President answered, "Well, it depends on whether he

addressed me as his father or as President of the United States. If it's the former I will deal with him shortly, but if it is the latter, then, as a citizen, he has the guarantee of freedom of speech!"[26] The President of the United States also knew how to preside at home. A father disciplines best when he is kind, firm, and consistent.

- *Before disciplining, he will gather all the facts.* A wise father finds out what's wrong and who is likely to blame before he acts. I was disconcerted when my five-year-old refused to eat a traditional breakfast that I prepared on Saturday mornings. About to chide her, I paused and asked: "Why don't you like it?" She stolidly replied: "Once I ate it and it had egg shell in it!" The matter was settled: Dad had been careless. I now do a better job cracking eggs than I did before!
- *Before disciplining, he will ask himself, "Have I clearly set the standard of behavior? Have I explained it? Is it fair? Is it fair to expect it under the present circumstances?"* An unclear, unfair standard flattens and destroys rather than lifts and improves. St. Paul reminds fathers to "provoke not your children to anger, lest they be discouraged" (Colossians 3:21). An unfair, unclear, and unattainable standard discourages a child. Fair standards are only fair when those who must meet them help in setting them. Include your child in rulemaking.
- *He will avoid physical punishment.* Tired parents find that spanking takes less time than reasoning and has a more immediate effect. However, a slap on the wrist or rear is only occasionally appropriate or effective. Those who would argue that an occasional switch puts a delinquent child on the right track fail to look down the road such action leads to. One rueful father said he was forty years old before he realized that there were modes of discipline

preferable to physical discipline. He had learned physical discipline from his father, who had learned it from his father, who had learned from his father. Apparently, none of these fathers knew that a soft voice six inches away from a child's nose and a hand on a shoulder, or even occasional isolation from the family or temporary denial of a privilege, works more effectively. If a child is aggressive and strikes, grab his hand. Tell him or her that hitting doesn't happen when you love someone.

- *In every instance, he will ask, "Is it punishment or patience that is needed here?"* Quick punishment usually does not ask questions, but patience does. Be patient with younger children and tolerant of older children. A tragic verse by Carol Clark Otteson sounds a familiar note:

> He dropped a dime
> in the cup of the blind
> Paid money to causes
> of every kind.
> Gave hours of time
> for those in despair
> And locked his son out
> till he cut his hair. [27]

I told my daughter, Sarah, who was habitually scruffy and dirty after a day's play, to clean up and shape up. I also asked the question, "Why are you always so!?" With full voice and candor she said, "Dad, it's because I'm closer to the ground than you are." Show patience. Ask questions before you punish. The answers may enlighten you.

Teach Me What's Important

Don't expect a mother, a school, or life itself to teach your children all they must know to survive and succeed. Fathers can teach values, good citizenship, and morality as well as anyone. One father described his short course for survival to his teenage family in four steps:

First: I urge my children to avoid sex and drugs.
Second: I insist that my children graduate from high school.
Third: I insist that my children get a job.
Fourth: I tell them to keep the job until they get a better one.

Each of this father's children has been successful, enjoys a high income, and is content.

Children need to hear their fathers' values. Proverbs 29:15 warns that "a child left to himself bringeth his parent to shame." Fathers need to voice basic values such as honesty, sharing, and self-control.

Two centuries ago, a critic of strong parental guidance was answered by Samuel Taylor Coleridge, the English romantic poet. Coleridge's friend insisted that a child's mind should not be prejudiced in any direction, so that when he came to his years of discretion and independence he could choose for himself. Coleridge listened and said nothing, but took the man to his garden. The man exclaimed, "This is no garden! There is nothing here but weeds!" "Well, you see," said Coleridge, "I did not wish to infringe upon the liberty of the garden in any way. I was just giving the garden a chance to express itself and to choose its own production."[28] A child deserves and needs parental guidance.

Fathers should encourage their children to work hard and bear in mind that the sleep of the laboring man is sweet. John W. Carr, former principal of the Friends Central School in Philadelphia, raised several sons who were strong, well-trained, and made a good living from the beginning of their careers. How did he do it? He taught them to work. He gave them three rules. The first was that when school was out in the summer, his sons had to find something to do for which they could be paid, if possible. The second rule was that his sons had to find something to do whether they received pay for it or not. The third rule, which he called "extreme unction," was that if a son could not find anything to do, he was to come to him and he would find something for him to do.

Dr. Michael DeCaria, psychologist and counselor, pays his daughter to pass him the tools while he tunes up the car. They learn a lot in those hours. His daughter learns mechanical skills, yes; but more importantly, she learns about her dad, and he learns about her! Dr. DeCaria adds that although the car always runs a little rough, parent-child relations run smoothly!

Fathers can teach learning habits. Learning can be easily encouraged but can be difficult to ensure when other factors are competing for your child's attentions. Children who have a regular and quiet place to study, with books and a dictionary, do better in school. It helps to have a father who encourages regular and undistracted study time.

Fathers should talk with their children about the future. Planning for high school and post-high school training and education is best done at an early age. Researchers and curriculum specialists note the appalling inability of many youths to discuss the future and their plans beyond a few afternoons or days. They are not future-oriented because they see the future more in terms of tomorrow than the coming years. National education fellow and curriculum specialist Mary Monroe observes that all children are at risk, regardless of economic status. Kids involved in drugs, sex, and suicide see only the immediate, the now, and the nearby. They do not see the future and the big picture. [29]

Fathers can steer their children down the path of education. How? By attending back-to-school nights and learning about their children's teachers. Avoid asking your children general questions like, "What did you learn or what did you do today at school?" Such questions usually trigger automatic responses like, "Nothing."

You can adopt three techniques to help maintain your

child's interest in school. First, make sure your child sees you reading. This allows your child to perceive that you approve of reading and do it yourself. Second, ask, "What did you discuss in Mr. Teacher's class today? Tell me about it." Asking specific questions reinforces that you take a genuine interest in what your child does and that you expect him or her to learn. Third, say, "That's important to know." Such affirmations drive home the fact that math or writing have value, that they can help pave the way to a promising future. Such affirmations stimulate desire and commitment to learn.

The father of comic Joe E. Brown took a more subtle approach to teaching what is important. Brown's father was a house painter. He was, however, more than a painter; he was an artful father who took pride in a full day's work for a full day's pay. Brown writes:

> We were on our way to the local ballpark to see a game on a weekend morning when we passed a house that dad had painted. "Now look at that," he exclaimed, stopping suddenly to stare at the house. "How could I have overlooked that?" I tugged at his coat-tail, impatient to get to the park. "Wait, son," he said, "there's a spot on Mrs. Forker's porch I didn't get. I must go back to the house and bring some paint." "But dad!" I cried, "we'll miss the game!" "The game can wait, son," he said. "Mrs. Forker paid me for painting her house." That was all he said, or would say on the matter. I was a grown man before I realized such examples were the foundation for my desire to give the best in every job.[30]

Teaching children to take pride in their work and to complete what they begin takes patience, but they will reap dividends for the rest of their lives. Earlier I discussed the powers of example, encouragement, and motivation. The benefits from these principles surface when a child takes pride in performing a job well. Fathers can instill these principles in their children as they teach them what is important.

Dad, Let Me Tell You What's Important

Can we learn from our children as much as they can learn from us? I believe so. Fathers who welcome good advice, wherever it comes from, will learn a lot from their children, although the directness of some of their counsel may be startling and occasionally hurtful. At times, a dad's ego is damaged—like a direct hit on a cruiser. Your child's honesty may sometimes be brutal, but if you take it in stride the catharsis will spawn better fathering. Three tools can prove useful as you seek to learn from your children: the personal interview, dealing at the child's level, and asking your child what he or she thinks of you.

A personal interview consists of regular but spontaneous, informal dialogue. Notice I said dialogue, not monologue. A personal interview can last as little as ten minutes or as long as an hour. It increases awareness on both sides. Slip into your son's or daughter's room or sit down at the kitchen table. My memory floods with conversations of driving my children to or from school when the radio was off and no one else was present. In such conversations, ideas or dreams for myself and for them were shared. Ask questions that cannot be answered with a yes or no. Say, "Tell me about . . ." or, "What is your feeling or opinion about . . . ?" Such an approach prompts a thoughtful response rather than a grunt. It communicates that you are interested in your child and his or her ideas.

Dealing at the child's level simply requires allowing your conversations with your child to follow his or her interests, friends, and activities—not yours. Most children hear enough from their fathers. Listen to your child's views. Let your child proceed at his or her level.

Finally, ask your children what they think of you. Ask how they think you are doing as a family. Ask, "Am I making it as a dad?" or, "How can I be helpful to you?" Ask your children what they would change in their relationship with you, and what they would do if they were in your shoes. Their answers can prove enlightening.

Practicing low-key dialogue encourages real listening. No judgments are being made. It binds fathers and children together, building marvelous bridges that they will pass over for the rest of their lives. Professor Phillip Flammer, former history professor at the U.S. Air Force Academy, was stunned to hear his son say in such a setting, "Dad, I've been afraid of you all my life." Dr. Flammer felt a ball of emptiness roll through his stomach, but was grateful for the candor which allowed him to begin allaying his son's fear. Flammer realized he had been guilty of showing his son what Robert Bly claims many children receive when father returns home at six after another long day at work, his disposition usually irritable and remote. In earlier, less complex societies, these lapses in temperament were offset by time spent teaching ropemaking, fishing, posthole digging, animal care, singing, and storytelling. Children do not do well when they receive only temperament and no teaching.[31]

On another occasion, a father's first interview led to a heavy subject. "Tim," the father began, "I'd like to discuss with you some of the facts of life." "Great, Dad," the boy replied. "What would you like me to teach you?" Another family remembers a similar setting where a father, whose son had never dated or shown interest in girls, grew concerned that his son was showing lively affection for a young woman who had considerable experience with dating and possessed savvy beyond his son's. The father's concern peaked, and late one night the interview ensued. "Don't you think you should date Elsie or JoAnn?" asked the father. "They seem to be more your speed and less aggressive than Toni!" The boy nodded, thought, then pensively answered, "But, Dad, Toni is as good a girl as I can get with the car we've got!" Needless to say, many things came out of that conversation—including a newer car!

Nearly ninety years ago, my uncle threatened to run away after a scolding from his mother. His father said, as if to shock the boy, "JB, go ahead! Let me help you pack." The surprised boy returned with his little suitcase and left for a long walk.

Night fell. He walked no further than the family barn, where he decided to sleep in the hay and get an early start. Shortly afterward, he heard a noise and held his breath, only to hear his father's soft voice below the hay loft say, "JB, are you there? Are you there? I've got some things on my mind and I am worried, too. Let's run away together!" They spent the rest of the evening talking and counting stars in the Milky Way through the cracks in the wood roof. They returned home at breakfast when the smell of bacon and eggs changed their runaway minds. This episode became one of the son's fondest memories of time spent with his dad.

Historian/philosopher Will Durant concluded from his studies of man, society, and the past that of necessity, government power arises and expands when parents and churches decline to teach their children. Teaching, motivating, showing sympathy, and disciplining are challenges that bring opportunities to prune the family tree and direct its branches toward the light. Heir conditioning and protecting family heirlooms can bring some of life's most profound, fulfilling personal pleasures to a parent.

Nine

Does Dad Need a Time-out?
Seeing Your Child on Five Dollars a Week

Baseball popularized the "time-out," the moment when the team reassesses its position in the game and forms a new strategy. Time-outs with your children can serve the same purpose. They allow you and your children to reassess, refresh, and foster good feelings. My neighbor, Alf Pia, is a successful father of five. He once said, while reflecting on how he raised his children, that he had only one regret:

I tried to spend time with my family *equally*. I did that well, we did everything together. We went to movies together, played ball, shared alike all that was good. What I failed to do was spend sufficient *time alone* with each of my children, separate from the rest. Personal relationships come on a one-to-one basis. That I would do differently—become a father who lifted each child out of the family for special treatment on a regular basis.

In *The Father's Almanac,* S. Adams Sullivan observes that fathering can become a peripheral issue for men, something we spend time on when we get a free hour. Would men be more conscious of how they fathered if they got a paycheck for their efforts? The fact is, we are being paid for it, but not in dollars and cents! Our payment comes in the form of wrestling matches and unsolicited hugs.

Too often, fathers fall back on common excuses for letting their children down, ranging from "I'm really too busy right now" to "I don't have any money" or "I'm too far away." Such excuses appear especially misguided when compared to what is at stake and what brings joy in parenting—positive memories with a child.

A wise person once observed, "For the best view of life, try climbing the family tree." Climbing the family tree requires taking a time-out. The time-out today is more vital than ever before. Pre-industrial and agricultural society structure allowed time for family members to interface with each other. Families were involved together in producing food and fiber. Prior to store-bought bread, wash-and-wear clothing, and fabric softener, family members conversed while they did their chores. The pursuit of convenience eliminated those chores and thus lessened opportunities for family time-out. Dishwashing, gardening, farming, and ironing once provided opportunities for conversation. Dreams, concerns, and anxieties were shared during the course of everyday living. It was a time when a child would enter the house and say, "What's cooking?" rather than, "What's thawing?" Reversing the trend toward tenuous relationships and the demise of familiarity within the family requires providing a conscientious, concerted infusion of time-outs.

You can provide the "infusion" for less than five dollars a week. What can you do on five dollars? You can purchase a plastic bat and ball, a handful of nails, wood, and glue, or kite string and paper. Five dollars can buy a root beer and hamburger and enough gasoline to drive to the edge of town to bird-watch, observe frogs, search for rocks, or take a short hike and clip cattails from a pond to have imaginary sword fights.

Five dollars a week will buy admission to a museum, a trip to the library, or launch a child into a Cub Scout or Explorer Scout project. City walks, walks in the woods, and a nature guide from the library will make you an instant expert on birds as well as on your son or daughter.

Singing, whistling, humming, reading a map together,

attending a high school ball game, and even changing washers on a faucet or washing the car are routine projects which take on new meaning if shared in the company of your child!

Time-outs should follow the child's interest, not just the father's. Young fathers will incline to physical or athletic activities, while senior fathers may incline to recline! Overcome inertia! Move your mass!

My father had limited health, but he used what little he had for us. His children and every child in the neighborhood went on a weekly truck ride. Our joy was just to sit in the back of a truck and wave and act silly. The only rule was to sit down and have a good time. Traffic laws frown on that today. That pick-'em-up-truck hauled countless Boy Scouts to meetings. The long line of bedraggled scouts receiving awards and advancements became the ideal time-out. Fathers and sons cheered each other and glowed with pride.

Want to leave an inheritance to your son and daughter? Leave lots of time for them—lots of time-outs.

Ten
Flexible Fathering and Children of Success

Children feel the demands of a father's career or hobby. The emotional impact of a workaholic or sportsaholic father on his children is as measurable as that of an alcoholic father. But, unlike alcoholism, the habits of workaholics or sportsaholics can be more easily broken and modified. The solution is flexible fathering.

Flexible fathering stems from the willingness of a "too-busy" father to admit that his kids deserve time in his life. "Too-busy" fathers may genuinely have little free time because their family expenses—health care, tuition, lessons, etc.—or business or job demand their attention. The prolonged working hours of an executive or even night work may be necessary.

Flexible fathering means playing six holes of golf instead of nine if time is a problem. Instead of spending all day at a fencing meet, find and attend the key events where your child performs. The effect is the same. My son was interested in golf. I played marginally. It took us three hours to play nine holes. We often came to the ninth hole well after dusk. Doing so cost us a lot of balls. I adjusted my philosophy to meet the need. Play what you can. It works for the very busy father.

Abraham Lincoln was a flexible father. He regularly played games with his sons. He received temporary reprieve and relaxation from the rigors and trials of his wartime presidency by sitting and playing with his sons, Tad and Willie.

Heber C. Kimball, a polygamous settler in the American West, had a string of sons from ten to fifteen years old. He wanted them to ride in the Founder's Day parade but was unable to provide shoes for them all. He knew they would be jeered by their friends if seen shoeless. He went to the blacksmith to solve his dilemma. The boys rode shoeless, but the public did not know because the blacksmith had set sideboards in their wagons which obscured the boys' feet. It was a solution dreamed up by a sensitive, flexible father.

Fathers who are businessmen can show flexibility by taking their children to the office or on business trips. Flexible fathering says to a son or daughter, "I count in my father's life, even though he is busy!"

Flexible fathering treats sons and daughters alike. As one daughter said, the most impressive thing about her dad was that he had four sons and one daughter and, in his eyes, she was as good at football, fishing, and field goals as any of his sons.

Flexible fathering avoids comparisons between children, instead emphasizing the qualities and strengths of each individual. Child psychologists remind parents that children are best served when we measure them by how they progress instead of by how they compare. Likewise, rewarding your children should be tied to their progress, not to how they compare with others. Flexible fathering recognizes that comparisons with siblings and friends stifle a struggling child.

Flexible fathering generates a relationship built on trust, time together, and mutual respect. It comes from love. It allows children autonomy as well as responsibility for their actions, and, when their actions seem misguided, it involves encouragement, helpful support, and feedback through conversation.

Alan K. Chalmer hit the mark when he said, "Happiness consists of something to do and something to love, and something to look forward to."[32] So is it with children. Men will find immeasurable joy in fathering as they show their children the flexibility that tells them they come first.

Eleven
Fathering From a Distance: Child Support is More Than a Monthly Check

The divorce of a man and woman need not lead to a divorce from the children. Partners need not poison each other in the eyes of the children, who, sad to say, too often become the real casualties of divorce.

Child support is more than a monthly check. A father can be an effective moral support to his child even when living across town or across the country. The muscles of parenting can be exercised through a letter or phone call. One separated father who has limited income writes regularly to his children, offering encouragement in school and in their part-time jobs. He encourages them to do housework, giving their mother, a business executive, much needed relief. His telephone calls are welcome. He is not a significant financial resource to the family, but is a coach and, more than anything else, a listener. A father must know that he cannot raise a child by remote control—his children need his companionship, even when it is offered from a distance.

When fathers are unavailable or unable to maintain contact with children, a prudent mother cultivates a mentor. A mentor is a capable, worthy male in the form of a friend, relative, or neighbor. A mentor is a role model, a cheerful support who is interested in the child's well-being.

Several years ago, a neighbor asked me if I would let her son accompany my son as he participated in school sports and social events. I was impressed that she sought me out and had confidence in me to fill the void in the boy's life. The boy thrived. Similarly, after my father died, my friend's father included me regularly in their family activities. My memory of seeing the Grand Canyon is doubly vivid because I remember both my friend and myself standing at his side as he described the canyon's fascinating history.

A mentor provides a jump-start. He provides the boost a child needs during life's critical transitions. Abraham Lincoln was, to use current parlance, "a child at risk." His mother died when he was ten years old, and the void in his life was disastrous. The family sank into squalor. With his father's remarriage came a stepmother who projected faith and confidence in the boy. She secured extra weeks of schooling for him and encouraged him in his dream to be a poet. She was his mentor, a woman he later referred to as "my angel mother."

"When one has not had a good father one must create one,"[33] wrote Nietzsche. Chuck Maack of Omaha, Nebraska, was one such "created" father. He drove a hotel van to and from the airport from 3:00 p.m. to midnight. Although retired, he filled the financial gap for his grandson, who won a swimming scholarship to Auburn University. The young man needed housing money, which Chuck cheerfully worked to supply in the absence of his grandson's father. Chuck Maack is an American hero of a different sort—a mentor to a promising boy.

Fathers who, for one reason or another, lose contact with a son or daughter can also serve as mentors by reestablishing their relationship with their child. At first, efforts to do so may feel clumsy. Like most beginnings, initial conversations may feel strained and awkward, focusing on superficial topics as father and child take each other's measure. However, with patience and persistent dialogue, deeper and more meaningful communication will eventually surface.

One father's alcoholism excluded him from his children's early years. He eventually sought treatment. Meanwhile, his only communication with his daughter was an occasional letter. His daughter described their first meeting after seventeen years. She recalled that when her father first visited her he simply held her hands as he talked. It provided a chance to catch up, blooming into the best conversation either had enjoyed in years. The daughter refused to harbor resentment. She determined to influence her biological father's life as he vowed to positively influence hers. She allowed him to catch up.

The economic position of a father is less important than the position he takes regarding his relationship with his children. Children seek their fathers even after the apron strings are cut from mother. The economic benefit of having a father is less profound than the guidance and emotional support he can provide. For example, many notable historical figures have thrived without having ample economic means in their childhood homes. Columbus was the son of a weaver. Cervantes, writer of *Don Quixote de la Mancha*, was the son of a common soldier, and the Greek poet Homer was the son of a poor farmer. Benjamin Franklin was the son of a candle and soap maker, and Shakespeare was born to a stapler. American poetess Phyllis Wheatley was born a slave but took strength from her black roots. The fathers of these outstanding people, regardless of their economic standing, took prominent roles in their childrens' lives, although much of their fathering was done from a distance.

Among the great inspirational stories of human history is that which tells of the love, separation, and reunion of ancient Jacob and his son, Joseph. Separated from his father by envious brothers, Joseph's love for his father continued from a distance, even through Jacob's fear that his son was dead. Their reunion in the face of starvation and famine affirms how strong parenting can positively influence a child's early years. Jacob nurtured the greatness in Joseph that eventually preserved the entire nation of Israel.

"Never let go, never let loose, never give up!" Such is the persistence of fathering. That is the attitude of my friend, Ron Smith, toward his grown children, who are scattered throughout the United States. On their birthdays, on holidays, or on impulse, he calls just to check in with them. For years, as they returned from dates at night, they checked in with him before going to sleep. "Now," says he, "it's my turn to check in with them." Tongue in cheek, he says, "We really are checking in with each other, and we love it." He's fathering from a distance!

Twelve

Fathers of Divorce and Substitutes

I recently spoke to the National Congress of Fathers and Children. The hall was filled with hundreds of fathers who, due to divorce decree, court order, or problems with their ex-spouses, were unable to visit their children. I felt the pain of their separation. These fathers were making regular child support payments and were meeting their legal obligations to their children. Yet they were isolated from them and in turn felt mounting frustration, even anger, at the legal system they felt had been unjust to the rights of fathers. I heard them assert that the children's rights movement must assert the child's right to have access to both biological parents, to have both parents involved in the child's life and well-being.

The love and concern that these fathers so ardently expressed for their children would move men across the world to reconsider that which most of us take for granted: the privilege of being an active, involved father. I thought of Thomas Jefferson when he wrote, "The happiest moments of my life have been the few which I have passed at home in the bosom of my family."

Though sometimes separated from their children, divorced fathers can still demonstrate love and caring for their children and take pride in their successes. You fathers without access to your children can and should send mail on a regular basis. This will help reassure your children that you will continue to love and be concerned for them. Call them by phone and occasionally send a cassette or video tape. Also, keep photocopies or duplicates of any communication. These can form a personal journal you can later share with your child.

A rewarding bond and relationship can develop from staying in close contact with your children. Your efforts to maintain close ties will strengthen your child's self-image, letting him or her know that you think of them more often than on only their birthday or at Christmas. Remember, you are building a relationship which will continue after the child reaches adulthood and relations normalize.

Children of divorce would suffer much less if parents could forgive and come to some degree of reconciliation for the children's sake. Such reconciliation requires that both spouses acknowledge that pain and hurt have occurred. In addition, reconciliation for the child's sake is furthered when each parent earnestly attempts to understand why the marriage did not work. Such efforts often bring divorced parents the strength or compassion needed to refrain from speaking negatively of an ex-spouse. Divorced parents should also ensure that their children understand that their divorce stemmed from problems with the parents and not the children. Doing so will help dispel doubts, second-guessing, and the child's feelings of incompleteness.

If you are a stepdad, you can bring great relief to your new wife. Her divorce has probably loaded her with greater burdens as a mother than she could have ever imagined. You can be the "relief pitcher" who saves the game for your new family.

All reports show that step-families are the most fragile and volatile family form. Removing the biological father weakens the family structure at its foundations. That said, consider this: A stepfather can be a stabilizing force in a step-home. Everything written in this book works for stepfathers as well as for biological fathers.

Stepfathers need to show extra sensitivity to their stepchildren. For example, stepfathers should avoid defaming their stepchildren's biological father. Even though the biological father may be absent, a child's stability and self-image are still tied to his or her biological father.

Try not to allow apparent indifference or animosity from your stepchildren to discourage you from being caring and supportive. Consider yourself the best dad in the world, and you will be!

Thirteen
Mrs. Dad

Twelve million mothers in America are raising their children by themselves. These mothers are offered no respite—there is no one to spell them when their patience wears thin or energy runs low.

My mother would have been counted among today's single mothers. Perhaps the best I can say about her situation is that somehow it worked out—not ideally, but it did work out. Raising children alone doubly taxed her mental, physical, and financial resources, but it also summoned up the best from deep inside her. Yes, somehow it worked out.

When my father died, he left children nine, thirteen, seventeen, nineteen, and twenty-one years old. There were no grandparents to turn to. Mother relied on common sense and grit, and tried to continue the same pattern of living to the extent that our diminished means of support allowed. She did the right things. She came to our school and church events, ball games, recitals, and concerts. At every turn, she increased her commitment to us. On Friday nights, she and I would go to a movie or a drive-in restaurant. She did not leave me to my friends exclusively. She became more active in my life, compensating for Father's absence.

My mother spent meaningful time with us. She taught us to

work alongside her, helping with housecleaning, dusting, window washing, and gardening. She expected all of us to participate in all the chores at home. When she returned to her former profession as a secretary, she did us all a favor: she expected the help from us. She got it, and things did work out.

What held my family together was that we spent more time together to fill the void my father's death left. We worked together even harder, and played together even more. Mother simply raised her expectations, and we rose to the occasion. She let us know she needed our help to make our life work.

My mother sought mentors for my brother and me, someone to teach us to fish and to help us do the work required on the small farm our father had kept. There were more than enough men available to help her, but she had to ask. Some mothers are reluctant to do that. Likewise, some men, when a mother asks them to mentor a son, speak sympathetically but never offer anything more substantial than their good intentions. As fathers, we should recognize the positive impact a strong male role model can have on a child's life. We must serve as mentors whenever we can!

Mother disciplined us, on occasion, either by scolding or withdrawing privileges. Once she took away a tennis racquet left on the back seat of the car because I had failed to lock the car. I thought it was stolen. Years later, she remembered she had hidden it away and returned it! After disciplining us, mother's usual cheerful demeanor returned. She carried no grudges.

Mother did not let fear of damaging her relationship with her children by administering discipline cloud her sense of responsibility to her sons and daughters. She consistently held us accountable for our actions. I now appreciate her commitment and determination, the strength she showed by holding her fatigue at bay regularly enough to intervene and give us the discipline and guidance we needed. I can now appreciate the resolve and energy that consistent, fair discipline requires.

Mother never complained about her plight, never asked for

sympathy. She only expected all of us to do our part. Occasionally she would say, "Your father wouldn't be happy about this." Invoking his name was enough to keep us in line, and at the same time allowed him to serve as a continuing influence in his children's lives.

Mother kept the essence of our father alive. She referred to him in positive ways. She recognized that our identities were inextricably tied to our father, that our self-worth stemmed from how we perceived him. So, too, should we recognize that speaking negatively of an ex-spouse only damages the children.

If you are a divorced or widowed mother and choose to remarry, and the children are deeply attached to their father, explain your need to them. Reassure them that your love for your new husband does not diminish your love for them. When my mother remarried, she set my mind at ease. She assured me that my father was a great man, and that no other man could replace him. She told me that the man she was marrying was a good, strong man, but that he would never take my father's place. For me, the distinction she so lovingly defined was profound. The memory of my father remained alive and untarnished. I gave my tacit approval to the marriage because my mother laid the groundwork for this new, good man's entrance into our home. It worked out for all of us.

Determined, committed "Mrs. Dads" will indeed find that things work out. You single mothers will watch matters fall into place as you strive to find mentors for your children and models for yourself. You will find that, as Seneca the Roman once wrote, "Adversity has a way of bringing talents and resources out of us that otherwise would have remained dormant." Here's to you mothers who are also fathers!

Fourteen
They'll Never Forget You: Hints of Endearment

Deep inside, children cry out, "I wish Dad would tell me he loves me." Perhaps the most fundamental of all human needs is to be loved. Fathers can change behavior through doses of love.

Fathers who regularly express encouragement and love can change their children's behavior. They validate the truism that the only way you can change your child's behavior is to change your own. Sincerely and freely expressing your love to your children will endear you to them and forever enrich their lives. The human heart, not the intellect, must be touched and convinced if human beings are to change.

Fathers can endear themselves to their children in countless ways. Here are a few I've discovered.

1. Nickname your children. When our first child was born, I responded to her cooing sounds by gently whispering, "Moogie, Moogie, Moogie." It fit my feeling of affection for her. In time, "Moogie" became a password of affection. I never call her that around friends or in public, but I still call her that occasionally. My mother called me "Senatahne," which she said means "little redhead." I cherish the thought and the name. She spoke it with affection.

2. Cultivate the sentimental. Have a favorite place to eat or get away to. Pick a song for each of your children that they identify with. Tell your child the song reminds you of her or him. "Raindrops Keep Falling on My Head," "Grandma's Feather Bed," "The Sun Will Come Up Tomorrow"—each of these has a meaning and memory for my children.

Plant or name a tree for a child. My parents did this. My brother had a horse chestnut tree, and my sisters had a hawthorne tree and a cherry tree. We even had a tree for our dog, who, by the way, put it to good use!

Each spring and fall cleanup, my children and I go to the landfill. Invariably we sing a song destined to be sung on rides to the dump, a version of Jimmy Durante's "Ink a Dink a Dink." We sing, "Come give your daddy a hug da da da da da da come give your daddy a kiss da da da da da da da." It brings us instant bonding and delight. We have many happy memories of the landfill!

3. Start a tender tradition. Give flowers on a birthday, a letter or note at the beginning of each school year. When we built our home, the children took nails and scratched their names in a freshly-poured concrete patio. Years later, our last child observed that her name was not in cement. Together we took a chisel and hammer and chipped "Emily" into the concrete. She looks at it wistfully and with pride and periodically says, "Remember when we carved my name in the concrete?" Tender traditions make indelible impressions, even in concrete.

4. Have a party at the drop of a hat. Parties change the atmosphere. Jump at every occasion to throw a party: the first snowfall of the year, when a storm knocks the power out, when the school teams win or set a record for the number of losses, or when the garage gets cleaned. Particularly memorable to me was successfully toilet training 2-1/2-year-old Becky while her mother spent a month in Europe. It was easy. We planned a short party that lasted all of ten minutes. We danced around a fire of burning Pampers, then had root beer floats. How could she forget the event and reverse her training after that spectacular send-off into a diaperless future!

5. Do spontaneous acts of love. A wink of approval at a recital or game, a thumbs up through a window, or a high five as you pass each other in the hallway are spontaneous acts of love. A gentle shoulder massage, unsolicited praise, a race up the stairs, or a quick game of "gotcha last" all say "I care for you!"

6. Share and tell. Lie on the floor, on the edge of the bed, or on the lawn and share with your children. Look at the stars and talk about your childhood, your fears, your first Christmas memory, how you felt when they were born.

7. Leave notes and love letters. Leave notes of affection in the bathroom, a drawer, a shoe, or a lunch sack. My daughter Becky practiced this artfully, leaving Hershey's kisses in strange places for family members—even once on the toilet seat! Hers was an example of giver's gain. She took as much delight in leaving the kisses as the family did in finding them.

8. Sacrifice. Put yourself in a service mode. When your child is pressed for time, offer a ride. Help press a dress, polish shoes, deliver a forgotten lunch to school, or give your last dollar, squeeze of toothpaste, or ounce of shampoo. Do your children's dinner dishes if they have a heavy test the next day.

9. Keep a "great moments" file. Keep a file of your children's unusual, precious, or dramatic expressions or actions. A "great moments" file focuses on character-building moments or expressions. My daughter Becky chased a man whose car she had slightly grazed in a parking lot. He responded with a joyful letter of appreciation. Refer to your children's great moments while they're present. It will give them a shot of self-esteem.

In addition to creating a "great moments" file, try giving a "Happy Warrior" award— some white elephant gift or curious award to recognize good deeds or actions in the past week. Our "Happy Warrior" award consists of sheet metal scraps welded together in the shape of Don Quixote standing ready to do battle.

10. Write a list of practical things and skills you want your children to learn. Teach your children these things yourself or have others teach them with your involvement. Tennis, bread-making, changing a top washer, knitting, and button sewing are all examples of what you can teach. In the process, your children will acquire more than just the skills you teach—they'll share in your conversation and insights, and, more importantly, learn that their dad cares and wants them to succeed.

11. Welcome your children's friends into your home. Four things will attract your children's friends to your home: ice cream, games, a playhouse, and, most importantly, parents who want them there. If your home is open and friendly, kids will come. If kids just drop in, you will know you are okay and accepted by them as a "safe" parent. It is a compliment to you.

12. Show and tell your approval. Praise your children frequently, openly, and genuinely. Do it in original ways. Tell them, "NASA is looking for the best earthling for a space shot. Can I send them your picture?" Or, "If you had been guarding Abraham Lincoln, he wouldn't have been shot."

These hints of endearment will deepen your relationship with your child, forming the ties that tug at your children's hearts when they question your love and interest. Despite assertions to the contrary, it is in men's nature to be nurturing. Fathers, make a commitment to nurture. Your children will adore you for it.

One early spring morning in 1949, my father slipped into our bedroom, gently lifted the covers back over our shoulders, and tucked us in. Seconds later, I heard a crash in the hallway outside the bedroom door. When we arose, we found Father lying face down on the floor. His last act before dying was to cover his children, to make them comfortable in their sleep. It was an act of endearment. I have not forgotten that.

Fifteen
Daddy Dividends: Things I Was Near Enough to Hear

"Daddy dividends" are the returns on investment that a father receives from being near enough to his children to overhear. Here are a few such "dividends" I was near enough to reap.

On sharing. David to Amy (age 8) at Easter time: "It's important that people share. Let's begin by sharing your Easter basket."

On peacemaking. Sarah (age 5) after listening to *West Side Story* and my interpretation of the tragic gang fight: "Daddy, wouldn't it have been safer if they had fought with their spoons?"

On reality. Emily (age 5) lost her tooth to be left for the tooth fairy. Sarah: "Emily, if you can't find your tooth, use a substitute—just leave a Tic Tac!" Emily: "The tooth fairy is not interested in Tic Tacs—he just needs teeth!"

On order. Amy (age 13) curling her hair, exclaiming: "This hair just doesn't make sense!"

On minorities. Lizzie (age 12) to David on his sharing the bathroom with his sisters: "David, you are a minority here. Leave the toilet seat down."

On self-interest or conflicts of interest. Becky (age 14) to me after meeting a family with four boys: "Dad, why don't we get together and do something with that family? Those boys need some caring, and besides, they are cute!"

On excuses. Lizzie (age 13) to me: "Well, Dad, I know you are upset with me, but you need to remember that I'm supposed to act this way. I'm in puberty!"

On misunderstanding. Emily (age 5) en route to a restaurant called Chuck-A-Rama: "Where are we going?" The answer: "To Chuck-A-Rama." Emily's response: "I don't want to go to chuck Grandma! I love her very much!"

On therapy. Emily (age 4) to me: "Dad, we haven't been on a vacation for a while. This family needs one again."

On paying attention equally. Lizzie (age 11) to me as I was volleying tennis balls to her and her sister, Becky: "Dad, send some to me, I'm still alive!"

On service to others. David (age 14) to my wife and me during a family conversation about helping others during the holidays: "I think we should do something different this year. Let's take Mrs. Grace (83 years old) skiing—it would be different for her!"

On Santa Claus. Emily (age 5): "You guys aren't Santa Claus. You always sleep in!"

On candor. Sarah (age 5) when I asked her what she liked best about a church meeting: "The end."

On death. Emily (age 3) to my wife at a funeral service: "Mother, the lady is in the box and they put the lid on. We've got to help her get out!"

On optimism. Lizzie to me while waiting to perform a musical at a rest home while a dozen elderly people in wheelchairs were being rolled in: "Dad, these people are in pretty bad shape . . . at least they won't get up and walk out on us!"

On growing up. Amy (age 4) to me (her shoes were tight-fitting): "Daddy, my shoes are on too much!"

On awareness. Emily (age 6) as her grandfather lay in bed a few days before his death: "I know Granddaddy is not doing very well, because whenever I talk with him he just says 'yes.'"

On kindergarten. Sarah (age 5) to me: "Kindergarten is for accidents. Things we do there don't count against us."

On success. Amy (age 7) to me: "Dad, I was the best one today in school . . . most of the kids were sick."

On perseverance. Sarah (age 12) in a note to me: "Dear Dad, I'm at Emily Grow's house. I got bored of waiting for you. I've had lunch and done my practicing. Thanks. Love, Sarah."

On trust. Emily (age 6) to me: "Dad, you gave me my own key to the hotel room. That means you trust me."

On experience. Sarah (age 4) to me while watching me struggle with a diaper: "Dad, let me help you. I know how it works. I was just there a little while ago."

On household budget. David (age 10) to me: "Dad, we would like a trail bike, but we can't afford one right now. Let's wait."

On being away. Emily (age 6) to me in a note on my pillow: "Dear Dad, I missed you so much. I am glad you are home. I and my Holy Ghost told me you are happy and would make it."

On caring. Sarah (age 10) to me when hit in the eye by a baseball bat: "I'm kinda glad it was me who it hit, because the next two people in line wore glasses, and the glass would have shattered in their eyes."

On gratitude. Lizzie to me as I was pulling covers over her at night: "Thank you, whoever did it!"

Sixteen
Patience: The Fatherly Virtue

Patience is the "ability to care slowly."[34] It is the ability to idle your motor when you feel like stripping your gears. It is the attitude that allows you to let the fruit ripen before you pluck it. It is the recognition and conviction that waiting will achieve more than force. It is the quality that I wish for more of in myself and in all fathers. Patience is the North Star in a father's universe.

Patience slips a noose over the tongue when it is about to fly loose. The tongue, not the sword, causes war. An uncensored tongue can quickly destroy the self-worth and confidence that take years to develop.

Patience is for fathers. If you are instructing your child, try to remember how clumsy you were the first time you tried to bat a ball, cast a fly, or write your name. Try to write with your non-dominant hand. Remember that, for most children, being a child is all "lefthanded."

Ignace Paderewski, the great pianist, was asked by an admirer if it was true that he practiced every day. "Yes," he replied, "at least six hours." "You must have a world of patience," the person replied. "No," said Paderewski, "no more than the next person. I just use mine." Fathers, use the patience you've been given.

A sweetheart makes a man a poet, but his children make him a philosopher. Patience helps develop the philosopher. When a mean impulse or thought boils to the surface, let it wait ten more minutes. It will soon go away. Remember to hold on. Hold fast and hold out, for, as Comte de Buffon asserts, "Patience is genius."

Seventeen
Resolve to Come Out and Play

A report entitled "Success Insurance for Youth: Home and School Insurance Against Failure" reaches some heartening conclusions for fathers to consider. First, it states that caring and supportive relationships with adults appear to be a significant element of childhood success. Without the right kind of socializing experiences with adults, children never completely mature, and the child can never grow up. [35]

The report also found that the best prevention against delinquency and dysfunctional behavior is good parenting. Similarly, it asserted that a child's parental relationship will most likely be his or her single most profound influence. Finally, the report found that ninety percent of all parents want to get involved and help children out of difficulty, but are at a loss as to where to begin. Parent training is a solution.

I have written this book for fathers, but why fathers and not mothers? First, an extensive amount of guidance on good mothering is available. In addition, mothers seem to consistently do better parenting than fathers. If fathers tried as hard as mothers, most children I know who are in trouble wouldn't be.

Fathers need only to resolve to be better fathers to win half the battle. Fathers need not fear failure, for failure will come only if they do nothing. Any effort toward better fathering reduces the risk of failure. Nothing will be lost if you make an effort. We must aspire to be good fathers.

"Accidents," as Dickens reminds us, "will occur in the best regulated families."[36] However, we can minimize missteps by thoughtfully directing our efforts and energy. Such efforts require simple resolve. Of that quality Ben Franklin wrote, "Resolve to perform what you might; perform without fail what you resolve."

As fathers, how do we summon the inner strength to give our children our very best? Perhaps as parents we would enjoy the moments, and the child, if we stopped to realize that the film of childhood can never be rerun for a second time—that one take is all we get. Such a somber thought might stir our resolve.

Freedom springs from resolving to do good. We cannot erase past mistakes or neglect, but we can surely strive to do better in the present and future. We can adopt the outlook of the ancient Roman who, when chided for his common birth, declared, "My nobility begins with me." Abraham Lincoln carried similar resolve, stating, "I don't know who my grandfather was. I'm much more concerned to know what his grandson will be." The brilliant Booker T. Washington put it this way: "I resolved that because I had no ancestry myself I would leave a record of which my children would be proud and which might encourage them to still higher effort."[37]

As a young man, my friend, Donald Brewer, made some important resolutions when the police brought his drunken dad to the doorstep one night. The embarrassed boy, when recognized, denied that he had been seen earlier by the officer at a Boy Scout meeting. Yet, something more positive happened that night. Donald vowed to go beyond his father, to earn respect for him and his family, and to tell the truth.

Of the three great forces governing our lives—environment, genetics, and personal response—the latter is all-powerful and all-determining. William James regarded the greatest discovery of his time to be the realization that human beings could alter their lives by altering their attitudes. Humanity's promise hinges on conscientious, positive fathering. The state of mind that leads to good fathering is one that fosters communion among spirits. Such a union of spirits is described by true-life characters in the movie, "Hannah's Diary." Hannah, a Czech resistance fighter against Nazi tyranny, was asked by her trainer whom she would save if forced to choose between her mother or the Royal Air Force pilots whom she had pledged to rescue. After a moment's contemplation, she replied, "I would save the pilot." "Why?" asked her trainer. Hannah answered, "My mother would forgive my choice."[38]

All of a man's life can be spent in the pursuit of fleeting goals, honors, and comforts, none of which will ever bring him more lasting comfort than the voice that greets him at the door when he returns from work, gleefully shouting, "Dad is home!" That same call can be echoed across the world by children of all ages, whether they are five or fifty. Every father should know the lasting joy that springs from the welcoming face of a waiting child.

The historian/philosopher Will Durant, recalling his search for happiness and success, says that his quest did not end as he would have expected:

> It came in a sudden fashion, not from my desire to reform the world, illuminating mankind's absurdities and injustices, neither was it found in the quest for knowledge. Rather, it came when I responded to the call of the little girl in my home who said: "Come out and play."
> For was that not the final purpose of my toil that I should be free to frolic with her . . . and so we walked and ran and laughed together and fell in the tall grass, and hid among the trees and I was young again. [39]

And so it is. Fathers, work *and* play. Work and play with your children whatever your age, whatever their way. Come out and play. Don't let the fire go out!

The Parable Retold

There is a tale, a parable of old men and young men.

And those who dared to leave the fire without leaving a log dared harder to return to the cave, since it took more courage to return than to leave and go into the night.

They returned to the place and laid a log on the fire, and all in the cave were warmed and sheltered.

And in their turn all placed wood on the fire.

And the fire never went out.

NOTES

1. Robert Bly, *Iron John: A Book about Men.* New York: Addison-Wesley, 1990, p. ix. Social historians report that the public's perception of what's wrong with their time often relates to rapid technology change, new inventions, and entertainment practices. The 1920s and 1930s are similarly accused with bobbed hair, the automobile, and the flapper characterizing the 1920s and joblessness in the 1930s. See also Paul Carter, *The Twenties in America* (New York: Thomas Y. Crowell Co., 1968); Forrest McDonald, *The Torch Is Passed: The United States in the 20th Century* (Reading, Mass.: Addison-History, 1968); and Mark Sullivan, *Our Times* (New York: Charles Scribners Sons, 1936).

2. Observation made at a meeting of the National Association of Counties, Human Services Steering Committee, March 1981.

3. Joseph Joubert, French writer (1754-1824) as cited in *Popular Quotations for All Uses,* ed. Lewis Copeland. New York: Garden City Publishing Co. Inc., 1942, p. 74.

4. The Old Testament, Malachi 4:6.

5. William Raspberry, "What Might Families Do When Families Crumble? Speak Truth!" in *The Washington Post,* citing Chester Finn, "Ten Tentative Truths."

6. Willard Rockwell, *et al,* "Thoughts on Father's Day," *Parade Magazine.*

7. James C. Humes, *Speaker's Treasury of Anecdotes About the*

Famous. New York: Harper and Row, 1978, p. 207.

8. Evelyn Mills Duval, *Marriage and Family Development.* New York: Harper and Row, 1985.

9. Robert I. Fitzhenry, ed., *Barnes and Noble Book Quotations* (revised and enlarged). New York: Barnes and Noble Books, 1987, p. 126.

10. American Planning Association meeting proceedings, Colorado Springs, Colorado, Spring 1990.

11. C. Merton Babcock, ed., *Moments with Father.* Hallmark Editions, 1974, p. 7.

12. *Ibid.*, pp. 18-19.

13. Old Testament, 1 Samuel 9:2.

14. Willie Morris, *et al,* "Thoughts on Father's Day," *Parade Magazine.*

15. Terry Lee Burnham, Ph.D., fireside address, Spring 1989.

16. Lawrence J. Peter, Ph.D., *Ideas for Our Time.* New York: Bantam Books, 1980, p. 17.

17. Morris Mandel, ed., *Stories For Speakers.* New York: Jonathan David, 1964, p. 37.

18. William Livingston Larned in Ralph L. Woods, ed., *Golden Treasury of the Familiar.* New York: Avevial Books, 1980, p. 454.

19. George Henry Shaw, a.k.a. Josh Billings, is the reputed author of this expression.

20. Judy Fetzer Edwards in conversation with the author, Fall 1986.

21. Dotson Rader, "I Want To Be Like My Dad," *Parade Magazine,* January 20, 1991.

22. Lydia Sigourney, "The Mother of Washington," Frank S. Mead, ed., *Encyclopedia of Religious Quotations.* New York: Books Incorporated, 1965.

23. Stephen Craig, in a sermon at his father's funeral, Salt Lake City, Utah, 1988.

24. Peter, *op.cit.*, p. 78.

25. Fitzhenry, ed., *op.cit.*, p. 77.

26. Humes, *op.cit.*, p. 183.

27. Carol Clark Otteson, quoted in a University of Utah forum, Salt Lake City, Utah, Fall 1989.

28. Humes, *op.cit.*, p. 154.

29. Interview with May Monroe and D. Michael Stewart, Ph.D., Salt Lake City, Utah, December 1989.

30. *Moments With Father, op.cit.*, p. 28.

31. Conversation with Phillip Flammer, Ph.D., Provo, Utah, June 1972. See also Bly, *op.cit.*, p. 97.

32. Donald O. Bolander, ed., *Instant Quotation Dictionary.* Mundelein, Illinois, 1969, p. 134.

33. Fitzhenry, ed., *op.cit.*, p. 263.

34. John Ciardi in Eugene E. Brussell, ed., *Dictionary of Quotable Definitions*. New York: Prentice Hall Press, 1970, p. 424.

35. *Success Insurance for Youth: Home and School Insurance Against Failure*. Salt Lake City, Utah: The Youth Enhancement Association, 1988.

36. Charles Dickens, *David Copperfield*, Chapter 28.

37. *Dictionary of American Maxims, op.cit.*, p. 20, and Booker T. Washington, *Up From Slavery*. New York: Doubleday, 1940.

38. "Hannah's Diary" (movie).

39. Lillian Eichler Watson, ed., *Light From Many Lamps*. New York: Simon and Shuster, 1951, p. 246.

Suggested Reading

There is an abundance of literature on family development, relationships, and issues. Like the Marine Corps, which is interested in "a few good men," I recommend a few good books for future reading to help fathers center themselves on their children.

1. Robert Bly's *Iron John: A Book about Men* (New York: Addison Wesley, 1990) stands out as a seminal book on what fathers might become as compared to stereotypes of the "tough man." Using images of the male in literature, religion, fairy tales and folk life, he explores the masculine person's ability to have deep feelings. There are many messages in his own use of symbolism to characterize the male and father role. To gain the full value of his messages requires re-reading and reflection. You will find it a pleasant exercise.

2. Dr. Victor B. Cline's *How to Make Your Child a Winner: Ten Keys to Raising Successful Children* (New York: Walder and Co., 1980) draws upon his vast research and clinical experience to give techniques for raising winning children. The winning child is a happy child, one who is confident, competent, and resilient. Active, responsible children can have success because their experiences have shown them how. The author focuses on self-esteem and a range of issues from TV and teasing to stealing. This is a valuable manual and resource to consult as you deal with the daily difficulties of raising children.

3. Dr. Hiam G. Ginott's *Between Parent and Teenager* (New York: The MacMillan Company, 1969) provides specific advice and demonstrates skills for handling the endless small events and sudden crises that are part of every parent-teenager relationship. Dealing with the adolescent issues of rebellion,

conflict, autonomy, identity, and more, he offers helpful methods of communication, healing dialogues, and positive approaches. He gives helpful insights on how teenagers view parents. Subjects such as driving, drinking, social life, and sex education are aptly dealt with in helping children learn to grow and adapt to change. It is a hopeful book which focuses on understanding and withstanding your teenager.

4. Dr. Fitzhugh Dodson's *How to Father* (Los Angeles: Nash Publications, 1974) is useful to fathers because it writes from the viewpoint of the father as he seeks to understand the stages of infancy, youth, and adolescence. He deals with issues relating to marriage, divorce, and remarriage. It, too, is a comprehensive and useful tool for parents—particularly fathers.

5. A stimulating book written on the function and role of families is Rita Kramer's *In Defense of Family: Raising Children in America Today* (New York: Basic Book, Inc., 1983). Writing from a journalist's perspective and experience, she asserts that only in a stable family with strong, affectionate parents does a child grow up with a sense of well-being, protected in a world that makes sense. Such a beginning provides the basis for flexibility of response that helps a child overcome difficulties later in life. Home is where values are taught. Conscience and resourcefulness can bring independence rather than dependency. The paradox is that strong authoritative figures can help their children become independent. While writing about child development, the author makes the case that through the traditional family, a democratic society gets the individuals it needs to survive.

6. A delightful book on the laughable side and perspective of being a father is Dr. Bill Cosby's *Fatherhood* (New York: Doubleday and Co., Inc., 1986). Cosby, who holds a doctoral degree in education, is one of America's funniest fathers. He has a special brand of humor, wisdom, and humanity. His anecdotes, based on his own experiences as a son and a father, tickle fathers but also help women to better understand the fathers and husbands in their lives. Cosby makes the point that

child-raising is still a dark continent, and no one really knows anything. You just need a lot of love, luck, and courage, because, says he, "you'll be spending many years in fear of your kids!"

7. I conclude with S. Adams Sullivan's *The Father's Almanac* (New York: Doubleday and Co., Inc., 1980), a book of practical advice and ideas for men who enjoy the fun and challenge of raising young children. Among its merits is a particularly useful chapter on providing a play yard and kids' rooms, with diagrams of how to construct climbing structures, swings and things. It is a book filled with realistic suggestions and tools for fathers who want to actively participate in the lives of their children.

About the Author

D. Michael Stewart holds a Ph.D. from Wayne State University and has held academic positions at six universities. His business is keynote speaking, training and consulting to national business, government, and educational organizations.

A tireless advocate of family values, Dr. Stewart organized and directed the United Nations International Year of the Family in 1995. This was the first global conference of mayors, local governments, and businesses in behalf of families. Earlier, he produced the acclaimed video *Building Your Family Dream*, which won the silver medal at the International Film and Video Festival in 1992. His award-winning Bridges program and corporate Adopt-A-School program have brought business employees to school sites, linking corporations, schools, and local governments to strengthen the self-image and life-skills of children and families at risk.

Dr. Stewart's interests include family, vocal performance, tennis, skiing, biking, running, and reading. He and his wife, Betty Lou, an educator and businesswoman, have six daughters and one son.